# RAILWAY HERITAGE

# THE
# LONDON &
# NORTH WESTERN
# RAILWAY

Mr J Whone
18 Grange Park Road
Bromley Cross
Bolton
Lancs
BL7 9YA

## LONDON & NORTH WESTERN RAILWAY.

| | | | | | | | |
|---|---|---|---|---|---|---|---|
| Capital | £119,000,000 | | MILEAGE OF ENGINES. | FUEL CONSUMED BY ENGINES. | WATER USED BY ENGINES. | NUMBER OF SPECIAL TRAINS RUN. | |
| Revenue—per annum | £13,880,000 | | | | | Passenger. | Goods, &c. |
| Expenditure do. | £8,670,000 | | | | | | |
| Number of Persons employed by Company | 78,000 | | | | | | |
| Do. do. do. in Locomotive Dept. | 21,100 | | | Tons. | Tons. | | |
| Miles operated on | 2,900 | Per Annum | 75,572,552 | 1,587,305 | 11,825,422 | 75,000 | 253,000 |
| Engines Owned | 2,984 | | | | | | |
| Carriages ,, | 9,200 | Day .. | 207,048 | 4,349 | 32,398 | | |
| Wagons ,, | 70,500 | | | | | | |
| Carts ,, | 5,100 | Hour .. | 8,627 | 181 | 1,350 | | |
| Horses ,, | 5,000 | | | | | | |
| Steam Ships ,, | 16 | Minute | 144 | 3T. 0c. | 22½ | | |
| Passengers carried annually | 87,000,000 | | | | | | |
| Weight of Tickets issued annually (which if placed end to end would in 10 years make a belt round the world 1¼in. in width) | 60 Tons | Second | 2½ | 112 lbs. | 840 lbs. | | |
| Tons of Goods and Minerals carried annually | 44,000,000 | | | | | | |

Lbs. of Water evaporated per Lb. of Coal consumed .. .. 7·45
Engine performance equal to a journey round the world every 3 hours.

| | | | |
|---|---|---|---|
| Number of Stations | 800 | Do. do. journey to the Moon in 28 Hours. | |
| Do. Signal Cabins | 1,500 | Do. do. journey to the Sun in about 15 Months. | |
| Do. Signal Levers in use | 36,200 | | |
| Do. Signal Lamps Lighted every night | 17,000 | Crewe Engine Works occupy 116 acres of ground, the covered area being 36 acres. | |
| Do. Accounts opened last year at Crewe for Special Orders for various Departments | 13,500 | Locomotive Department, | |
| Annual Value of work done at Crewe for various Departments | £939,000 | CREWE, Nov. 13th, 1901. | |

Card issued by the Locomotive Department, Crewe, on 13 November 1901,
showing general statistical information about the company.

# Railway Heritage

# THE
# LONDON &
# NORTH WESTERN
# RAILWAY

## A 150th anniversary tribute
## to the 'Premier Line'

### Edward Talbot

Silver Link Publishing Ltd

First published in July 1996

British Library Cataloguing in Publication Data

A catalogue record for this book is available from the British Library

ISBN 1 85794 086 5

Silver Link Publishing Ltd
Unit 5
Home Farm Close
Church Street
Wadenhoe
Peterborough  PE8 5TE
Tel/fax  (01832) 720440
e-mail  pete@slinkp-p.demon.co.uk

Printed and bound in Great Britain

# ACKNOWLEDGEMENTS

Without the willing help of many friends and fellow enthusiasts it would not have been possible to produce this book. In particular, Philip A. Millard provided virtually all the detailed information about carriages, while W. G. Allen, Don Best, Jim Boulton, Eddie Bray, Michael Bentley, Peter Davis, Chris Eccleston, Bill Finch, Richard D. Foster, Arthur Gould, Lance King, Barry Lane, Malcolm Lewis, John Pritchett, Peter J. Stead, Clive Taylor and Ken Wood all went out of their way to provide information and help of various kinds. I am grateful to them all for their patience in answering my questions and for their willingness to dig deep into their notes and memories.

Unfortunately, as is often the case, the original photographers are now largely unknown. Those who are known are as follows: W. Leslie Good, page 71 (both), reproduced by courtesy of W. T. Stubbs; H. G. W. Household, page 125 (lower); H. J. Patterson Rutherford, pages 96-7; G. W. Smith, pages 124, 126 (upper); Leslie J. Thompson, page 61 (reproduced by courtesy of W. G. Allen); and A. E. L. Thorne, page 16 (upper) and 28 (lower).

Other photographs have been kindly provided from their own collections by the following gentlemen: W. G. Allen, pages 63 (both), 64 (upper) and 65 (lower); Don Best, pages 79, 80 (lower) and 81 (both); S. V. Blencowe, page 75; Eddie Bray, page 99 (upper); Roger Carpenter, page 74 (lower); Bruce Ellis, from the A. G. Ellis collection, page 110 (upper); Bill Finch, page 15 (upper), 73 and 74 (upper); Bernard Matthews, page 20 (upper and middle), 21 (lower), 22 (upper) and 29 (upper); M. C. Musson, page 68 (both) and 69; J. H. Price, page 22 (lower); F. W. Shuttleworth, page 36 (upper) and 70 (both); and Ken Wood, page 39 (upper).

The remaining photographs come from my own collection, which has been built up over many years.

Finally, the London & North Western Railway Society (membership enquiries: 2 Carpenters Wood Drive, Chorleywood, Herts WD3 5RJ) played an important role as always in facilitating contact with like-minded enthusiasts. Its friendly meetings are always enjoyable and fruitful, and its Journal, edited by Mike Williams, is excellent.

To all these gentlemen and to anyone else who has helped in any way, I extend my sincere thanks.

# CONTENTS

Probably the only surviving picture of a McConnell 'Patent' 2-2-2. The engine is No 47; built by W. Fairbairn in 1854, the class of 12 engines was intended to work a proposed 2-hour service between Euston and Birmingham. They were designed to burn coal rather than coke; the firebox incorporated McConnell's patent combustion chamber and was divided longitudinally, having two firehole doors, which no doubt complicated the task of the fireman; the chamber itself extended into the boiler barrel. In the smokebox there was a steam 'drier' - McConnell appreciated the advantages of what is now called 'superheating', but failed to develop it. Originally, Coleman's springs, consisting of three rubber discs separated by ½ inch iron plates encased in castings above the axles, were fitted to all wheels, but in this photograph they are now retained only on the leading wheels, leaf springs being visible on the driving and trailing wheels. Another unusual feature of the design was the cylinders, which were inclined downwards at the front, the opposite to normal practice. The photograph can be dated between 1 April 1856 and May 1862, as it was only during that period that the engine carried the number 47.

# INTRODUCTION

In the golden age before the First World War, when railways enjoyed a monopoly of transport and were at the height of their development and influence, the London & North Western Railway was the greatest of all the British companies. Its main lines served five of the largest cities in England - London, Birmingham, Liverpool, Manchester and Leeds - and all the major industrial conurbations except Tyneside. It provided through services to Scotland via Carlisle, to Ireland via Holyhead using its own steamships, and even to America via Liverpool. It was the largest joint stock corporation in the world and thanks to its absorption of the Liverpool & Manchester Railway it claimed to be 'the oldest established firm in the railway passenger business'. It also claimed to have the 'finest permanent way in the world', a claim that was never disputed, and it was rightly known as the 'Premier Line'.

The London & North Western Railway came into existence on 16 July 1846 when the Royal Assent was given to a Bill authorising its formation. It was formed by the amalgamation of three companies: the London & Birmingham Railway, which had opened on 17 September 1839; the Grand Junction Railway, opened on 24 July 1837; and the Manchester & Birmingham Railway, opened on 10 August 1842. The Grand Junction Railway, which was so named because its main line from Birmingham to Earlestown linked the London & Birmingham with the Liverpool & Manchester, had already amalgamated with the latter in 1845. Thus the three companies were natural partners geographically since they served the four major cities of England. The Manchester & Birmingham, incidentally, ran only between Manchester and Crewe, where it connected with the Grand Junction; its name derived from an earlier scheme to link Manchester with Birmingham, which was proposed soon after the London & Birmingham Railway was promoted.

The 1840s were a period of rapid expansion of railways, which eventually culminated in the 'Railway Mania'.

The LNWR, however, was essentially immune to this excess, since it was able to expand by leasing or acquiring companies, many of which its constituents had subscribed to or helped to promote, so were already being built. Its constituents were all highly profitable from the outset, and although the cost of expansion and the need to meet competition reduced the level of profitability and of dividends, the company nevertheless remained in profit and maintained its dividends when the 'bubble' burst elsewhere.

The company's system, therefore, expanded rapidly. By means of the North Union Railway, the Preston & Lancaster Railway and the Lancaster & Carlisle Railway, the LNWR reached Carlisle on 17 December 1846, the joint station there being opened on 1 September 1847. The Trent Valley Railway was opened on 1 December 1847 and provided a direct route between London and the North, avoiding Birmingham, which had already become something of a bottleneck. In fact, the Trent Valley had already been taken over by the London & Birmingham before the formation of the LNWR. In the same year the company absorbed the Huddersfield & Manchester Railway and the Leeds, Dewsbury & Manchester Railway, thus gaining access to the lucrative traffic of West Yorkshire. Then in 1850 the Chester & Holyhead Railway was opened throughout (the Chester & Crewe Railway had already been bought by the Grand Junction in 1840).

Thus by 1850 the main lines of the LNWR were already in existence and the only other major expansion was the 'Invasion of South Wales', which took place in two main stages. First, in 1862 the LNWR acquired the Shrewsbury & Hereford Railway, jointly with the Great Western Railway, so gaining access to the coalfields of the eastern part of South Wales, west of Abergavenny, as well as to Bristol and the West of England. Secondly, the Central Wales Railway was opened on 10 October 1863 and was worked by the LNWR from the outset, being bought outright in 1868. This line, with various extensions and acquisitions, gave access to Swansea and West Wales.

While these were the outer limits of the system, a constant process of development and expansion took place so as to develop the company's business, to secure the traffic available in its area and to allow it to compete successfully with its rivals. Secondary routes and branch lines were built or acquired, especially in the West Midlands, the North West and the West Riding, and the company gained access to Oxford and Cambridge. Agreements were also made with other companies for joint lines and running powers, and by this means access was obtained to the East Midlands coalfields, to Nottingham and Doncaster, and to Sheffield and Hull.

From the beginning much effort was also expended on increasing the capacity of the system by enlarging stations, goods sheds and marshalling yards. A notable feature was the adoption quite early of four tracks on main lines, to enable fast trains, such as express passenger and goods trains, to be segregated from slower trains such as stopping passenger trains, slower goods trains, mineral trains and pick-up goods trains, thus avoiding delays. Four tracks were in operation between Stafford and Crewe from 1876 and effectively between London and Rugby from the opening of the Northampton loop in 1882. The North Wales line between Chester and Llandudno, much of the main line between Crewe and Preston, and the Leeds line over Standedge also had four tracks. It was planned to have four tracks throughout on the Trent Valley line, but the First World War interrupted the work and it was never resumed.

Major works were undertaken at Crewe around the turn of the century, to enlarge the station, build avoiding lines for goods traffic under the North Junction and to improve facilities for goods traffic in Basford Hall and the Tranship Shed. Another project delayed by the war was the remodelling of the junctions at Chalk Farm just south of Primrose Hill tunnels in London, but this was completed after the war. It is an indication of the comprehensive measures taken by the company to facilitate the flow of traffic that in the electrification of the West Coast Main Line during the 1960s, flyovers were needed at only two points, Rugby and Weaver Junction. Another was built at Bletchley, in connection with a plan for reorganising goods traffic, but soon fell largely into disuse.

After the amalgamation of 1846, it took some time before a settled organisation of the new company was established. The management of such a large enterprise as a railway, spread out over a large area and with only primitive means of communication available, presented considerable difficulties to the Victorians, but fortunately the company had several competent administrators, of whom Captain Mark Huish and Sir Richard Moon are perhaps the best known. The success of their efforts can be measured by the continued profitability of the company.

Perhaps one reason for this was that throughout its existence the LNWR pursued a policy of self-sufficiency to a far greater extent than is fashionable today. Not only did the company build its own engines, carriages and wagons, but it also manufactured many of the other things that it needed. Certainly this was partly because it believed it was cheaper to do so, but probably, at least originally, another major factor was the absence of suitable suppliers. For example, in the establishment of the steel works at Crewe, the LNWR was a pioneer in the country as a whole. Then, having acquired the capacity to produce steel, it was only sensible to make the fullest use of it, to produce not only rails but also steel for engines and for every other possible purpose. Another example of self-sufficiency is that the company also produced its own wooden buildings in standard sizes, for stations, signal boxes, platelayers' huts and the like.

Eventually large workshops were concentrated at Crewe for engines, at Wolverton for carriages and at Earlestown for wagons. The Locomotive Department centred on Crewe had far wider responsibilities than building and repairing the company's stock of engines. Within Crewe Works were the steel works, brick works, signal works, grease works and departments dealing with matters outside the works. For example, the works also constructed, installed and maintained the hydraulic machinery that operated the lifts at the company's stations and goods warehouses and drove the capstans at innumerable points in goods sheds, yards and sidings, and at steam sheds.

The Locomotive Department was headed by a succession of great engineers and administrators. Francis Trevithick was the first Superintendent at Crewe and, following the advice of Joseph Locke to standardise, he built only one basic type of engine, known later as the 'Old Crewe' type, in two variants, one for passenger and one for goods.

His successor, John Ramsbottom, built six classes but continued the Crewe tradition of standardisation by using the same major components in several different classes of engine. Some 943 of his 'DX' Class 0-6-0 were built by 1872, a record for one class of engine that was never broken in Great Britain. The same cylinders and boiler were used in his 'Newton' Class 2-4-0, and the same cylinders in several other classes also. Ramsbottom expanded Crewe Works and installed the steel plant. He was also a prolific inventor, being responsible for many improvements to the steam engine, which made it a much more practical machine. He also installed the first water troughs in the world. These were a great advance on busy lines, since they reduced costs in several ways. They were sited where supplies of good water were available, or could be treated easily, reducing boiler costs, and they enabled engines to be equipped with smaller tenders, reducing the weight that had to be hauled about unproductively.

Ramsbottom, who retired in 1872, was the last Crewe

Superintendent to be appointed from outside. His successor, F. W. Webb, was trained at Crewe, as were all subsequent holders of the office, so the traditions laid down in Ramsbottom's time were followed for the rest of the company's existence. Moreover, many of them were followed abroad also. Far more engineers were trained at Crewe Works than could be employed there subsequently by the LNWR, and many of them went to railways established by British companies overseas, in India, for example, and other parts of Asia, in Africa and in South America.

It was under the superintendence of F. W. Webb that the LNWR was developed into the form in which it is largely remembered today. He developed Crewe Works to the stage where it became, in the words of *The Railway Magazine*, 'the greatest locomotive works in the world'. He pursued the standardisation methods of Ramsbottom to the point where a far greater degree of standardisation was achieved than by any other British railway before or since. He built engines that had a style developed from his predecessors and followed by his successors, which made them instantly recognisable as North Western, even apart from their distinctive black livery, which he had adopted. Under his superintendence, Crewe produced its own style of signals and much of the equipment at stations, such as nameboards and seats, which gave the railway its own distinctive and unique appearance.

The achievements of F. W. Webb, the 'King of Crewe', were enormous, as he more than any other man made the LNWR what it was. It is unfortunate, therefore, that modern popular writers often ridicule him on the basis of the defects of some of his compound passenger engines and choose to concentrate on this one point while overlooking the many great achievements of his long career. Certainly, he failed to produce a really reliable compound, although not all his compounds were failures, and certainly he failed to produce engines capable of coping with the great increases in train loads that occurred at the turn of the century. At that time, however, he was already

at an age when he would have long been retired today, and it was a measure of his success in managing Crewe Works that the directors failed to replace him earlier and only did so when he became seriously ill.

Today the LNWR is largely remembered for its black engines and its splendid passenger carriages. It produced the first all-corridor train in Great Britain in 1897, and soon afterwards introduced its 12-wheel stock for the 'Corridor', for dining and sleeping saloons. The stock it built for the Royal Train and for the 'American Specials' is rightly famous, and indeed in general the company is justly associated in the popular mind with the excellence of its passenger services of all kinds, not only its major expresses. It should not be overlooked, however, that the LNWR was also a major carrier of goods traffic of all kinds. Express goods services gave overnight transits to all parts of the system, taking meat, for example, from Scotland, woollen goods from the West Riding and imports through the docks at London and Liverpool. At the other extreme were long trains of coal, especially between the Midlands and London, as the company served most of the main coalfields in England and Wales. In between were mail trains, milk trains, parcel trains, mixed goods trains and pick-up goods trains serving every wayside station.

Today little remains of the splendid railway that was once the LNWR. The route itself survives, still with long stretches of four tracks south of Crewe especially, and still shows something of the vision of those who built it. Of the old Euston there are only the lodges, the war memorial and the statue of Stephenson himself, and of Crewe Works only a small fraction of the shops remain. Fortunately, however, many excellent photographs of the company in its heyday have survived. It is hoped that, on the 150th anniversary of the formation of the company, the selection contained in this book will form a fitting tribute to a magnificent railway and to all the men and women who worked to make it what it was.

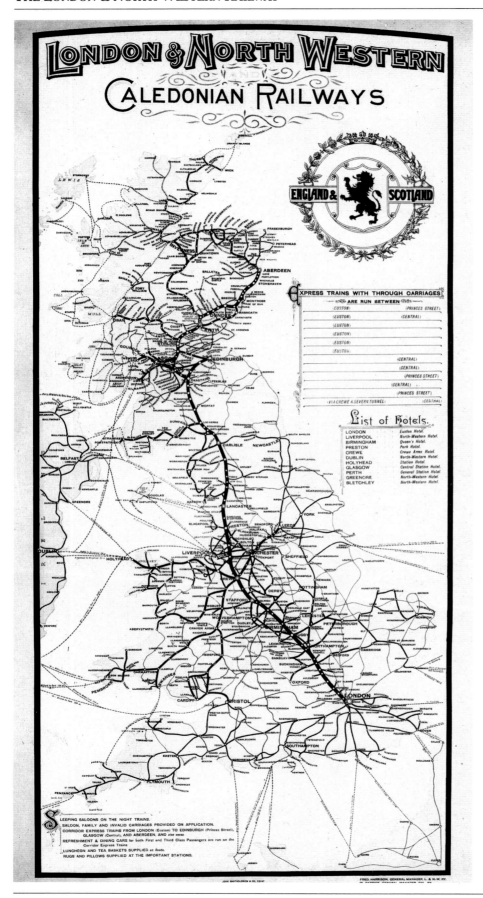

*Left* Map of the London & North Western and Caledonian Railway systems and connections in the period before the First World War.

# Euston

*Above* A view of the Doric Arch at Euston some time in the late 19th century, and from the attitudes of the cab drivers, it seems to be a warm summer afternoon. Surrounding the courtyard beyond the arch is the Euston Hotel, and beyond the building seen through the arch is the Great Hall. The main departure platforms were on the left, suburban and parcels platforms beyond the Great Hall, and the arrival platforms on the right. The small lodge to the left of the arch, with a clock, contained a post office. Originally, the arch led straight to a carriage road, with the one departure platform on its right

All the buildings in this picture were demolished in the 1960s to make way for the present Euston station. While it is to be regretted that such fine buildings as the Doric Arch and the Great Hall were not preserved in some way, it has to be conceded that there was an overwhelming case for a completely new station. A 1938 account sums up the situation that had prevailed ever since 1838: 'Nobody remembers the time when Euston Station was not being altered or added to in one way or another'. Despite the new station, things have not really changed today.

*Right* The room card issued to W. L. Harris when he stayed at the Euston Hotel in 1922, reproduced here at actual size. The lettering on the original is in brown and the room number is written in pencil; the card itself is quite thick rather than being just of good-quality paper. The 1922 *Railway Year Book* carried an advertisement for the company's hotels at Euston, Birmingham, Liverpool, Bletchley, Crewe, Holyhead, Greenore and Preston, and stated: 'Hotel Porters in Red Coats meet the Trains and Boats and convey visitors' luggage free to and from the Hotels'.

A view of the Board Room in the Great Hall, Euston, about 1895.

A scene on the departure side at Euston in 1904, with a Liverpool (Riverside) train on the right and another down express on the left. The vehicle on the right is dining saloon No 127 (for details see page 109); the carriage number is displayed at the top of the inside of the doors, to help passengers find their compartments again after leaving the coach at a stop. The style of these numbers is reminiscent of engine shed plates; however, they were not in fact enamel plates as on the engines, but were simply black-and-white transfers. On the vending machine in the centre of the picture the horizontal signs all read 'Sweetmeats'; the two centre vertical ones read 'Chocolate', and 'Butterscotch'; and the other four read 'Fruit Jellies', 'Edinburgh Rock', 'Cocoanut Macaroons' (sic) and 'Chocolate Cream'.

*Above* Dining saloon No 290, which was built at Wolverton on capital account, photographed at Euston probably very soon after being completed on 20 March 1903. It was among the first of the famous 12-wheel diners that many regard as the most handsome of LNWR carriages, 65 ft 6 in long, 9 feet wide and with clerestory roof. Originally it was built as a 2nd/3rd Composite and was intended for Euston-Manchester and Euston-Liverpool services; hitherto dining facilities had been available only to 1st

Class passengers. The labels in the windows at the nearer end read: 'Dining Compartment For Second Class Passengers'. When 2nd Class was abolished in 1912, No 5290 (as it had become in the 1910 renumbering) was reclassified as a 1st/3rd Composite on Diagram 35A, seating 12 and 18 respectively. It became LMS No 10455 at the Grouping, and No 269 in the 1933 scheme, but was sadly withdrawn in 1935 along with others of this Diagram that had been made redundant by new LMS construction.

The elaborate livery deserves close study as the paintwork seems to be unblemished, the roof in particular still being pristine white. Nowadays it perhaps seems foolish for the LNWR to have painted the roofs of its carriages white, as they were certain to become dirty very quickly in the smoke-laden atmosphere of the steam age. There was good reason for it, however, as flake white paint was the most durable paint known at that time.

*Left* A poor picture technically, but one of some interest, since it shows a subject of which very few pictures exist - the first compound tank engine, converted by Mr Webb from a 'Metropolitan Tank' in 1884. It is seen here taking water at Euston in the early 1890s and has probably worked in on a suburban passenger train. When first converted it was shedded at Willesden and was used on stopping passenger services in the London area, including the 'Mansion House' trains, but it later went to Buxton, with the other compound tanks.

# Camden Bank and shed

*Above* A 'Claughton' descending Camden bank past the carriage shed on the approach to Euston about 1922. It has sandpipe windshields, dating the picture in the late LNWR period, 1920-2, and Ross pop safety valves, so must be one of the batch of ten built new with these valves early in 1920; almost certainly it is No 194. A six-wheel brake van leading was still a not uncommon sight at this period, and may well be serving its normal function as a parcels van; but it is possible also that it is conveying a coffin, such vans often being employed for that purpose when necessary, in which case that would be the only traffic it contains.

*Below* At the other end of Camden bank, 'Precursor Tank' No 653, which was one of the first batch, being put into traffic in September 1906, nears the summit with a down semi-fast to

Bletchley in 1924. Despite the load, nine 50-foot suburban carriages and at least two more bogie vehicles at the rear, no banking engine is provided.

The nine coaches form Euston-Watford Set No 6. A large number of these arc-roof suburban carriages, 50 feet long and 8 feet wide, were built around the turn of the century and made up into coupled trains (LNWR parlance for 'set trains') in various formations for use in the London, Birmingham, Liverpool and Manchester areas. The leading vehicle is a six-compartment Brake 3rd to D345, No 6607 or 7532. The Euston-Watford trains originally consisted of 12 sets built in 1897-1901 with the formation: Brake 2nd, Compo, 1st, Compo, 3rd, Brake 3rd. Set No 6 was the last of the initial series built in 1897 on steel channel-section underframes, which can be identified by the round ends of their headstocks, clearly visible in the photograph. The trains were originally gas-lit, but were soon converted to Stone's electric lighting system, with two battery boxes on each side under each vehicle.

Over the years the formations of many of these sets changed considerably, which was unusual for the LNWR where most coupled trains stayed together for most of their lives. Two of the original carriages of Set No 6 were destroyed in an accident at Willesden on 5 December 1910, and spare vehicles were substituted. In April 1919 the set was made up to nine carriages using similar arc-roof vehicles from disbanded Broad Street-Watford sets. The second carriage is one of these; it is a later version built on the 1901 pattern bulb-iron section underframe identifiable by its square-ended headstocks. Set No 6 was repainted in LMS livery in November 1927 and was later assigned to Extra Train No 65.

A down express, double-headed by two 'Jumbos', passes the north end of Camden shed in about 1907. The somewhat empty appearance of the shed would no doubt please the shareholders, since most of the engines are out on the line earning their keep. On the left is part of Chalk Farm station. This area was transformed by the Chalk Farm widening, which was begun before the First World War but was delayed by the war and was completed only in 1922. New tunnels were driven under Primrose Hill and burrowing junctions constructed to separate the Watford electric lines from other traffic. Chalk Farm station lost its main-line platforms and was then served only by the Broad Street line.

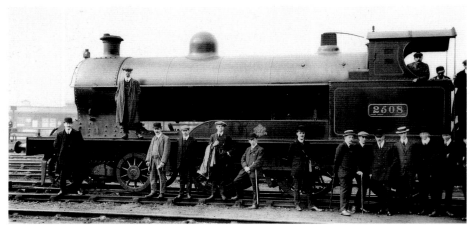

A group photograph of a visit by the Railway Club to Camden shed in May 1908, with '19-inch Goods' No 2508 forming the backdrop. The man in the bowler hat, directly below the numberplate, is Fred W. Dingley, shedmaster at Camden. His grandfather was foreman in charge of the erecting shop at Crewe in the 1860s, and several other members of the family achieved prominent positions on the LNWR. After the Grouping he became Superintendent of Motive Power Western Division (South). As the Railway Club was a semi-professional organisation, a direct comparison is unfair, but the dress of these Edwardian 'gricers' is certainly smarter than that of their modern counterparts!

'Claughton' No 1161 *Sir Robert Turnbull* passing the north end of Camden shed on a Euston-Liverpool 'Belfast Boat Express' about 1920. It is one of the first batch built in May-June 1913. The first carriage is a 57-foot Brake Van to D307D, one of the conversions from vehicles built for ambulance trains that never entered service as such because the war ended.

# The 'City-to-City' express

'Renown' Class 4-4-0 No 1913 *Canopus* at Dalston Junction about 1910-14, taking the line to Broad Street with the 'City-to-City' express from Birmingham (New Street). This train was put on to counter the increased competition on the Birmingham line that result-ed from the opening by the Great Western Railway of its shorter route via Bicester. On the right is a North London Railway suburban train.

Another Birmingham express hauled by the same engine, 'Renown' No 1913 *Canopus*. The first vehicle is a cove-roof double-ended corridor slip composite to D208. Though the official photograph of *Renown* on first con-version shows a steel-framed 3,000-gallon Whale tender, most of the class seem to have been fitted in service with wooden-framed 2,000 and 2,500-gallon Webb tenders, as built for the 'Alfred the Great' Class com-pounds from which many of the 'Renowns' were converted.

# Mansion House services from Willesden

In the late 19th century intensive suburban passenger services were developed between Broad Street, Willesden Junction (where interchange was made with main-line services), Kensington, Mansion House and East Croydon. As electrification spread in the early 20th century the steam services were modified and cut back. This view shows a train for Mansion House pulling out of Willesden Junction (High Level) some time in the late 1890s. It is hauled by a Webb 4 ft 6 in 'Mansion House Tank', and for some reason the fireman has gone into the bunker. There is a white diamond route indicator in the bracket on the engine chimney; many photographs show engines with these brackets, but only those of Mansion House trains or allied services, for which a special system of route indicators was employed, show them with indicators in position. It seems therefore that they were used only on these services. The LNWR headcodes at this period used the engine lamp sockets.

The view looking south-east along the up platform at Willesden (High Level); clearly a train for Broad Street is expected. This photograph was reproduced with a comprehensive article on the working of Willesden Junction station in *The Railway Magazine* in 1897.

The entrance to Willesden Junction station. The large board reads: 'Frequent trains to Dalston, Broad Street, Mansion House, Kensington, Victoria, Kew, Richmond, Waterloo, Herne Hill, Clapham Junction & Croydon, Royal Mail Route to Birmingham, Liverpool, Manchester, Chester, North and South Wales, Carlisle and all parts of Scotland and Ireland. Sleeping Saloons [conveyed?] on Night Mails and Dining and Drawing-Room Cars on Day Express Trains'.

A Mansion House train in the platform at Kensal Rise in 1914. The trains were made up of standard sets, enabling signs to be erected advising passengers where each class of carriage would stop, as on the right. Because they were constantly subjected to the smoke-laden atmosphere of London, the carriages were constructed of varnished teak, and so became commonly known as the 'brown trains'. The change from the normal LNWR livery was decided upon in 1890 'to avoid the cost of continual repainting' and to keep the trains in 'clean and better condition'.

The exterior of Hampstead Heath station about 1910, with a full array of LNWR and North London signs.

*Above* A Mansion House train somewhere en route, possibly near Kensington, hauled by No 781 in the late 1890s. The destination board on the bunker reads: 'Willesden Junction for North Western Main Line and Mansion House'. These boards are believed to have had white letters on a black background. Again, there is a white diamond in the chimney bracket.

*Below* A general view of Kensington (Addison Road) station. The carriages on the right are joint 'Great Western & Metropolitan Railways', while a goods train from Willesden seems to be waiting for the road on the centre line.

A Mansion House train standing at East Croydon on the London, Brighton & South Coast Railway, hauled by 'Mansion House Tank' No 785 about 1900; it has an oval route indicator board in the chimney bracket. The nine-coach sets built specially for these services comprised, as in this picture, left to right: Brake 2nd, 2nd, 2nd, 1st, 1st, 3rd, 3rd, 3rd and Brake 3rd.

Another view of a 'Mansion House Tank' at the same spot, with a diamond route indicator in the chimney bracket. Though the engine appears to have been in service for some time and the paintwork is no longer new, it is well cleaned and polished.

'Mansion House Tank' No 663 standing at Willesden Junction in the late 1890s, though not on a Mansion House train. A special batch of Webb '4 ft 6 in 2-4-2 Tanks' was built for the Mansion House trains and so acquired this nickname. They were fitted with condensers, by means of which the exhaust steam could be passed to the side tank at the control of the driver (the pipe and control rod are visible in this picture). Because this caused the feed water to heat up, and injectors do not work with hot water, a feed pump driven by an eccentric on the rear driving axle was fitted in the cab, an unusual place for such an item. A Webb injector was also provided, on the right-hand side of the firebox.

# Willesden, Harrow and Stanmore

*Right* 'Precursor' No 622 *Euphrates* in the main-line station at Willesden Junction with an ambulance train of London & South Western Railway stock about 1916. It is facing in the up direction but seems to have stopped short of the platform or has reversed along it; the crew are apparently waiting for a signal from the rear, so probably some shunting movement is being made. The engine was never superheated and was scrapped in 1927.

*Below* The view looking north from Acton Lane overbridge, just north of Willesden Junction shed, in 1893. The rural surroundings come as a surprise and serve as a reminder that extensive yards for goods traffic were already provided at this period and had been laid out away from built-up areas. The two lines on the left are the low-level goods lines that pass beneath the main lines to link Willesden Junction down sidings by the shed with the slow lines, without blocking the fast lines, which are the two tracks next to them. To the right of the fast lines are the slow lines, and to the right of them are the high-level goods lines, which lead to City Goods, south of the bridge; next comes Willesden Yard itself. The signal box centre right is Willesden No 8, which controlled the high-level goods lines in the yard only. All the main-line points and signals in the foreground were worked by Willesden No 7 box, which was on the down side south of the bridge. The long through crossing from the down side to the up must have been bolt-locked between the two boxes.

The two shunting engines are a '17-inch Coal Engine' 0-6-0 and a 'Special Tank'; the latter has no cab, normal for this period, and has a white diamond on the back of the rear spectacle plate. White diamonds were regularly displayed on wagons as the LNWR company 'logo', but this is only the second picture showing one on an engine, the other being that of 'DX' No 568 *Stewart* outside the Old Works at Crewe, believed to have been taken in 1861. Little is known about these diamonds on locomotives, partly because of the extreme scarcity of photographs of engines from the rear.

A general view of an accident at the north end of Willesden Yard, probably about 1908. There has been some sort of derailment, probably on the up slow line, and one wagon has been dragged out of the wreckage by means of a chain. The engine on the breakdown train is a 'Special DX', beyond it, with another crane, is perhaps an 'Experiment' 4-6-0, while approaching on the up fast is a 'Precursor' on an express. It has just come through Wembley for Sudbury station (now Wembley Central) and is about to pass Sudbury Junction signal box.

*Above* The celebrated '6 ft 6 in Jumbo' No 955 *Charles Dickens* passing Harrow & Wealdstone with the 4 pm express from Euston to Manchester on 31 May 1902. From its completion in 1882 this engine worked the 8.30 am express from Manchester to Euston and the 4 pm from Euston to Manchester regularly six days a week. It completed one million miles on 12 September 1891, in nine years and 219 days, a record equalled by no other engine in the world, and on 5 August 1902, shortly after this photograph was taken, completed two million miles. Its total mileage of 2,345,107 was never exceeded by any subsequent steam engine on the West Coast route, not excluding Stanier and BR Standard 'Pacifics'.

*Below* A general view of the outside of Stanmore station, terminus of the branch from Harrow, about 1909. The station is particularly attractive, with fine ornamentation on the roof.

Two views of the Harrow-Stanmore branch train at Stanmore on 15 June 1909. The engine, No 999, was originally a '4 ft 6 in 2-4-2 Tank', but was converted with No 1001 to a 2-4-0 tank in 1908 for the Red Wharf Bay branch in Anglesey; another three of the class were converted at the same time. The vehicles are, next to the engine, 50-foot Composite No 654, built in 1898 and originally in Liverpool-Bootle Set No 4, and 50-foot Composite No 443, built in 1897 and originally in Broad Street-Watford Set No 2. They were converted in 1909 for motor-train working and remained together a long time. In 1911 they were in use as an Earls Court set, later as Willesden No 15 Set, and later still as Motor Composite Set No 32; they were still fitted with rod motor apparatus on withdrawal in 1933, when they were converted to dormitory coaches. The station is particularly attractive, with fine ornamentation on the roof, numerous posters and enamel advertisements, and superb lamps.

# The 'New Lines'

A 'Precursor Tank' pulls away from Hatch End on the down slow line about 1906 with a train largely consisting of 50-foot suburban stock. This rural scene is shortly to be transformed by the construction of the 'New Lines' between Willesden and Watford on the right; they were opened throughout on 10 February 1913 and were at first worked by motor trains. The new stations served only by these lines were a major factor in the urbanisation of this part of London. Extensions to Broad Street and Euston, and a connection to the Paddington extension of the Baker Street and Waterloo section of the London Electric Railway (now the Bakerloo line) were added later, and the whole service was electrified.

A Bowen Cooke 'Superheater Tank' on the up fast line just south of Harrow & Wealdstone probably in 1912; the 'New Lines' are being laid in the foreground. The train is a Euston-Holyhead set, these engines apparently having a regular working, for some reason, on an up Holyhead train from Rugby. The first vehicle is a cove-roof end Brake, regularly used in Holyhead trains.

A construction train on the 'New Lines' about 1912. The up line has been completed and is being used by a '17-inch Coal Engine' with a train of stone, which is being unloaded to form the foundation for the down line.

A motor train leaving Kenton on the up 'New Line' about 1915, before electrification. The leading vehicle is Driving Trailer No 2938 of Diagram M33. It was built as 3rd-1st Composite No 559, conforming to D187, in 1899, and was included in Liverpool-Bootle Set No 1. The set was split up in 1909 and No 559 was converted to a driving trailer for the Stanmore branch. The driver's compartment was made from a former 3rd Class compartment and one of the 1st Class compartments became a 2nd, the layout being: driver, 2nd, 2nd, 2nd, 1st, 1st, 1st. No 559 was renumbered 2938 on 30 September 1911 and included in Earls Court Set No 1, a motor train set that comprised: 2938 (M33), 1743 (M62), engine, 888 (M62), 4034 (M34); 2nd Class became 3rd in October 1916. In 1919 this set was split up and 2938 was assembled into the two-coach motor set seen here, for use on the St Albans branch.

The other vehicle is Trailer 3rd No 698 of M62, which was one of the earliest 50-foot arc-roof suburban carriages of D296 built in 1896 for Euston-Watford Set No 4. This set was split up by 1916, and 698 was converted to motor use by the fitting of rodding apparatus but was otherwise unaltered.

In 1921 this set was re-designated Compo Motor Set No 3, but by 1924 698 had been replaced by cove-roof 3rd No 1437 of M57. No 2938 became LMS No 9511 on 7 April 1925 and 17972 in the 1933 scheme; it was withdrawn in March 1937. From 1924 to 1927 No 698 formed Compo Motor Set No 16 with Driving Trailer No 3660 of M24. It was renumbered LMS 5345 on 20 August 1925 and was withdrawn in 1942. Both vehicles are electrically lit on Stone's double battery system and were so fitted from new.

*Above* Another motor train just north of Kenton, probably in the summer of 1916, behind '4 ft 6 in 2-4-2 Tank' No 816.

*Below* A 'Rebuilt Precursor' just north of Kenton with an 'American Special' from Euston to Liverpool (Riverside), probably also in the summer of 1916. The train consists mainly of 65 ft 6 in stock with a 57-foot Brake 3rd to D313A leading and possibly another at the rear; the fourth vehicle is an eight-wheeled Kitchen

Car in the same style as the 65 ft 6 in stock. Electrification work is proceeding on the 'New Lines'; the down line seems to be finished (the insulators are still new and white) and conductor rails are lying beside the up line, waiting to be fixed in position. Although this picture is very similar to many others of down LNWR expresses at this location, it may well be unique, as photographs of 'American Specials' and of 'Rebuilt Precursors' in LNWR livery are very rare indeed.

# Bushey troughs

*Above* The first of the 'Precursors', No 513 *Precursor*, with the down 2 pm 'Corridor' in 1904.

*Below* A 'Precursor' takes water with a down express about 1905. The load is typical of those reliably hauled single-handed by these engines, and which had required double-heading a few years before.

Three somewhat unusual views of up trains on Bushey troughs about 1900, most pictures being taken nearer track level. All the engines are well cleaned, two being immaculate, although all are merely humble 0-6-0s and working quite ordinary trains. Their condition may be taken as typical of North Western engines at this period.

*Above left*  A Northampton-Euston excursion train hauled by a 'Special DX'; it seems to be going very well despite its years.

*Left*  A '17-inch Coal Engine', No 2315, on the up slow line with a typical mixed goods train. The fireman is on the right-hand side of the footplate waiting to raise the scoop, using the lever on the front of the tender.

*Above*  From the opposite side of the cutting another 'Special DX', No 1289, approaches with a goods train, also on the up fast line. The white diamond denotes an express cattle or express goods train. On 1 January 1903 the LNWR began to use the standard head-codes of the Railway Clearing House, following which boards such as the white diamond were done away with.

# Watford to Berkhamstead and Cheddington

A 'Precursor', probably No 2585 *Watt*, on an up express approaching Watford Tunnel about 1907. The fireman has rigged his 'dodger', a sheet of sacking or canvas to reduce draughts, between the engine and tender. Although these are referred to as being in common use by knowledgeable writers such as Dr Tuplin, this is the only known photograph showing one in position. No doubt it will be removed before Euston, to prevent it being seen by an inspector!

At first sight a fairly ordinary view of a 'Teutonic' Class three-cylinder compound on a down express in the early 1890s, but on closer examination one that contains several interesting features. The engine is in original condition, before the frames were cut back at the front end, and has several parts burnished, such as the smokebox door wheel and handrails, the chimney cap, the brass cylinder covers, and the spectacle frame in the cab; it also has a burnt smokebox door. In addition, the station nameboard has reflections in it, as if made of enamel rather than being painted, and reads 'Boxmoor and Hemel Hemsted' (sic).

*Above* An unidentified 'Jumbo' awaiting departure from Cheddington with an up passenger train consisting of 12 six-wheeled carriages. At least one through carriage from Aylesbury is about to be added at the rear.

*Below* At the other end of the station about 1904 a train is waiting to leave on the down fast line headed by a 'Jubilee' Class four-cylinder compound. The platform for the branch train to Aylesbury is on the right.

*Left* A train for Aylesbury standing in the branch platform at Cheddington, probably about 1895. The engine is 'Special DX' No 2034, which is nicely turned out, and the train, the Aylesbury No 1 Set, is a typical 'coupled train' (that is, a close-coupled branch-line set) of the 1885-1900 period. Such trains were commonplace on the many ordinary services of the day and for that reason were rarely photographed. The carriages at either end are 30-foot five-compartment 3rds, which have been converted to Brake 3rds, with the guard's entrance doors at the extreme ends; the two centre carriages are 28-foot Composites dating from about 1869.

*Below left* A much later view at Cheddington, looking south along the main down platform, with the Aylesbury train on the right. It is probably waiting to connect with the down train that is expected shortly; a train is also signalled on the up fast. The date is 25 May 1934, but except for the carriage the scene is still essentially LNWR.

# Bletchley and Bedford

Bletchley shed on 4 September 1917. On the left 'George the Fifth' Class 4-4-0 No 1799 *Woodcock* is receiving attention from a youthful gang of cleaners (who are probably too young to be firemen); the man standing on the left is a fitter. On the back of the tender is what is presumed to be a 'Not To Be Moved' sign, a length of timber with a white diamond at either end. This is one of the very few photographs known, showing such a board (another can be seen on page 39). Next to the 'George' is 'Big Jumbo' No 506 *Sir Alexander Cockburn*, which seems to have already been cleaned. On the right is a 'Cauliflower'. Six-road sheds like this, made up of two three-road units, were not common on the LNWR.

Another view at Bletchley on the same occasion, taken at the side of the shed, looking north and showing many fascinating small details: the shovels and fire-irons leaning against the 'coal hole', the bucket, the large pile of ashes, the water tank, with its level indicator near the bottom, the stylish lamps with their white-painted ladders, and the whitewashed coal stack. *Woodcock*, now well cleaned, is posed on the left, and also posed are the men with the coal tub on the tender of the 'Cauliflower' on the right. This engine carries shedplate 3 (Bletchley) and the tender number is 356. As was quite common, the tender numberplates of both engines are painted black all over.

The coaling arrangements seen here were typically LNWR and are well described by Jack Nelson in *LNWR Portrayed* (Peco, 1975). Loco coal wagons were pushed up a ramp into the coal stage, which was often surmounted by a water tank, and unloaded either firstly on to the floor or directly into tubs. A loaded tub was pushed against a kind of large metal flap, pivoted across the opening in the side wall of the stage, and so forced it outwards into a horizontal position. The tub was then pushed out on to the flap and its contents tipped into the tender.

*Above* This picture, taken possibly at Crewe South, is perhaps the only one in existence in which a 'Not To Be Moved' board is quite prominent - it has been hooked up out of the way on the wall on the right. The engine, No 1865, is an unsuperheated 0-8-0 of Class 'D'; it was converted from a Webb three-cylinder compound of Class 'A' in February 1909 and is seen here probably soon afterwards.

*Below* A general view of Bedford (St Johns) goods yard on 4 April 1914 with what looks like a '17-inch Coal Engine' shunting. The second wagon in the second train from the right seems to be carrying a carefully stacked load of bricks.

# The Newark Brake Trials

In June 1875 brake trials were held at Newark on the Great Northern Railway; the LNWR entry was fitted with the Clark and Webb chain brake. These two photographs, perhaps taken near Wolverton before the trials, show the train left for the trials, show the train that was sent. The engine is 'Precedent' No 2187 *Penrith Beacon*, which is quite new, having been completed only in April. It carries an early version of the lined black livery, with full red, cream and grey lining on the boiler bands, lining on the lower edge of the tender frame, including the spring pads, and no coat of arms on the splasher. The carriages are all 30 ft 6 in long, four Composites (with large coats of arms, which seem to

be of the type used later on engines) and one flat-sided Brake Van, on the edge of the roof of which is the wheel for the Harrison communication cord.

Usually, to operate the chain brake, the driver wound in the cable with the winch on the left-hand cab side-sheet; this indicated to the guard in his van that he should apply the brake, which was really a sort of handbrake, connected from one carriage to another by chains (they are just visible in the picture). However, this may be an early form of it, as the engine does not have the familiar vertical stanchion on the front of the left-hand side of the tender.

# American Base Ball Clubs Special Train

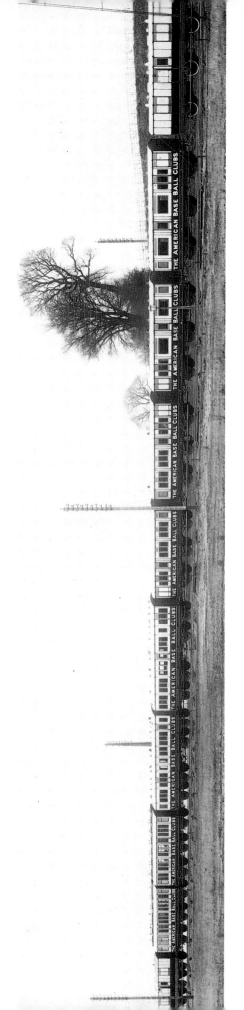

Two views of a special train provided for American Base Ball Clubs, which were presumably touring the country. The engine is 'Problem' Class 2-2-2 No 667 *Marmion*, and the date is probably 1889 (the engine has the vacuum brake pipe round the front of the cab, to operate the brakes on the train, no front vacuum pipe and oil axleboxes on the tender; the latter two features were both introduced on *Teutonic* in March 1889). From left to right in both pictures, the carriages are: 32-foot Brake Van No 210 (which are built in 1884; a pair of 34-foot ladies' and gentlemen's saloons of 1882-9 (which are lettered 'DINING SALOON', the nearest being No 53); a pair of 42-foot ladies' and gentlemen's saloons; two 32-foot family saloons dating from 1882; two 32-foot family saloons of more modern design built in 1886 (they must be Nos 141 and 142, as they were the only two to be mounted on a 22-foot wheelbase underframe, radial at one end); and a 32-foot Brake Van. Presumably the stock was specially lettered for the tour and had to be repainted afterwards.

## Wolverton Works: LNWR carriage stock

*Above* A general view of the interior of the body shop on 9 January 1894, with 30 ft 1 in carriages under construction.

*Below* A general view of the interior of the paintshop, also on 9 January 1894. The first carriage on the left dates from the late 1860s, the one in the middle at the end is a 32-foot passenger Brake Van, and on the right is a 30 ft 1 in five-compartment van, which must be new.

The fitting shop at Wolverton Works, also photographed on 9 January 1894.

A very rare close-up photograph of the type of main-line carriage built in large numbers in 1871-7. It shows Luggage Tri-Composite No 1126, which was built in 1871. The photograph was taken in April 1881, almost certainly after the carriage had been fitted with the simple vacuum brake; the cylinder is visible, at a slight angle, in front of the centre axle, but in general the chain brake arrangement of such parts as brake blocks, rodding and so forth is retained. The springs and spring blocks are an early type, the centre wheels do not have swing shackles, which were called for from 1881, and the axleboxes are grease-lubricated. The buffers are the longer later pattern, with ogee headstocks; when they were replaced by the square-ended. The rubber blocks on the underframe, supporting the body, can be clearly seen. The doors have short individual steps, with a continuous footboard below, and the

luggage doors are narrow (3 ft 6 in) with commode handles, as opposed to the later locking type. The waist panels are painted white (they were slate from 1885) and carry the word 'LUGGAGE'. The quarter light frames are the Saltley pattern, slightly sunk below the surrounding panel. The Harrison cord is threaded through the rings on the edge of the roof, its end hanging down for connection to an adjacent vehicle. The oil lamp tops on the roof are also an early type. The underframe is very fully lined out, with lining even on the bolt heads, the axleguards, the ends of the headstocks and even inside the headstocks! The coat of arms is the type used on engines from 1880 and generally thought to have been designed for that purpose.

By the mid-1880s these carriages were reduced to branch-line and local service in 'coupled trains'. Broadly, they were supplemented in the 1890s (that is, put on the duplicate list) and were broken up in the first decade of the 20th century.

*Top left* Another interesting example of carriage practice in the 1880s, Fruit and Milk Van No 193, which was built in 1886 and broken up in 1913. It is 25 feet long and 7 ft 3 in wide, and is straight-sided. The underframe is of wood, with a bulb-iron strengthening plate on the solebar and body support brackets. Again the brake arrangements are basically as in the Clark and Webb chain brake, but with a vacuum cylinder replacing the chain mechanism. The centre axle has no provision for side play (that is, swing shackle links are not yet fitted). On the roof the tops of the oil lamps are just visible, along with strangely shaped ventilation cowls that were much in vogue in the early 1880s. The photograph was taken about 1901, as the lower foot-board has been removed and replaced by a short step, a steam-heating pipe has been fitted and the communication cord is still in position.

In the left background is the body of a 14 ft 6 in horse-box, a very numerous type in the 19th century; all were withdrawn in 1898-1901.

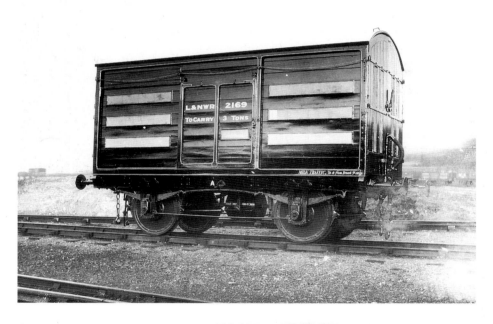

*Middle left* Covered Carriage Truck No 2169, photographed at Crewe in 1901. It is 21 feet long by 7 ft 10 in wide and 8 ft 10 in high, and is allocated to 'MILK TRAFFIC, To & From Broad St only'. It has grease axleboxes (doubtless changed to oil within a few years), the old-pattern underframe and horizontal vacuum cylinder, and Harrison cord. To provide extra ventilation for milk traffic, some of the body planking has been cut away and covered with perforated zinc. It was built in November 1886 as No 169 and was supplemented in 1900, 83 of the type being built between 1884 and 1892; only those still in capital stock in 1915 appear on D448 in the diagram book. Although built as covered carriage trucks, many were altered to milk vans within ten years of construction. Others were allocated for the permanent use of various builders of private carriages (and later motor cars), while later still many were branded as motor car trucks. At the Grouping, 22 were in capital stock, becoming LMS Nos 4610-31, with others as duplicates; five survived in 1933, with three duplicates, and the last was scrapped in March 1937.

*Bottom left* A more modern example of a 21-foot Covered Carriage Truck to D448, built on a steel channel underframe. It was originally No 22, became 11022 in the 1910 renumbering and obtained a 0 prefix when supplemented in 1913; at the Grouping it was allotted LMS No 04051, but was scrapped before receiving it. This photograph was taken at Crewe on 6 August 1913. The vehicle has been rough-ly shunted, resulting in damage to the end doors. It has the 1901-pattern oil axleboxes and a single lamp iron on the end. It is dual-fitted - the vertical arrow on the solebar indicates the release valve for the Westinghouse brake, while the 'A' indicates the vacuum-brake release. The 'S' shows the position of the steam-heat drain-trap valve (although the steam-heating pipe has been removed). The lettering is white, but the body is lined out in the 'economy' style.

*Top right*  Combination truck No 12211, built in 1916 to D444A; it is in wartime livery with lettering in white paint instead of gold. The main difference from the pre-war D444 is the use of hinged double doors in the side instead of sliding doors. Steel wheels came into use, in place of the Mansell variety, from 1913.

*Middle right*  To supply gas for recharging gas-lit carriages at points not equipped with gas-producing plants, a fleet of 'portable gas receiver wagons', of several designs, was used. No 4 was built on a 21-foot under-frame and carried 128 cu ft in the two tanks. It was based at Nuneaton and became LMS No 05390. The livery is black with white lettering.

*Bottom right*  A minor case of rough shunting! A tank wagon, converted from an old engine tender, has been forced on top of 16-foot loco coal wagon No 45637 of D64. The latter is lettered 'When empty to MOSSFIELD COLLIERY, LONGTON, NSR, via COLWICH.' and 'When loaded to WOLVERTON GAS WORKS'. The two vehicles have different types of couplings: the tank wagon has the original type, with the shackle secured by a pin through a hole behind the hook, and the coal wagon the later standard type, with a slot behind the hook to take the flattened part of the first link, which was then worked round into position. In the background is some old rolling-stock, including supplementary 3rd No 3943, which is part of a close-coupled set in the all-brown livery used for workmen's trains; the old-style ogee-shaped headstock is visible.

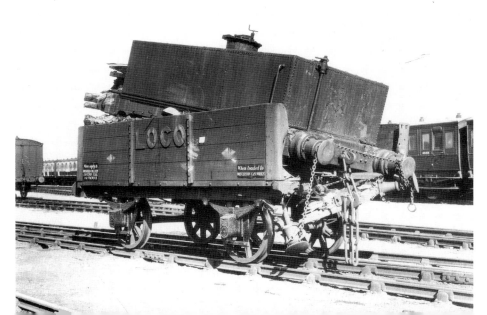

*Left* A view of Composite No 855, which was damaged beyond repair in the accident to the 12 midnight express from Euston to Liverpool and Manchester at Stafford on 12 March 1906. It was one of 30 bogie vehicles to D157 built in the first half-year ending in November 1894; the rest all survived into LMS days. The photograph was taken at the south side of Newport Road bridge, looking west. The steam breakdown crane is the first one to be owned by the LNWR and the only one to be constructed by the company itself, having been built at Crewe on the instructions of Mr Webb about 1900.

*Below* The interior of 42-foot twin dining saloons with clerestory roofs, July 1890. The carvings, mythological scenes and magnificent decoration in general seem to be no less splendid than the interior of a Royal Saloon.

Two 57-foot saloons, Nos 234 and 235, built in 1908 for the Llandudno Club train.

London-Rugby Set No 1, one of four similar sets of 50-foot lavatory stock built in 1905. The vehicles are, from right to left: Lavatory Brake 2nd No 182 (D326), Lavatory Composite No 52 (D153), Lavatory 1st No 64 (D102), Lavatory 3rds Nos 368 and 33; and Lavatory Brake 3rd No 163 (D326). These vehicles formed permanent sets that were not intended to be split up. Thus the vacuum brake pipe running below the footboard was coupled between adjacent vehicles at the side rather than in the centre, and only some of the vehicles had dynamos and cell boxes. The set was reduced to five vehicles at about the Grouping by the removal of the Lavatory Composites, but then continued as a set well into LMS days, probably into the late 1930s, and all but No 163 survived into BR ownership. Originally the brake compartments had four windows in the ends, as seen here, but the two centre ones were later removed, as they were frequently broken by the boots of staff climbing on to the roof. More sets were built for the London-Rugby/Northampton services in which the brake ends and the composites were extended to 54 feet in length.

On 1 January 1909 the LNWR effectively took over the North London Railway. This train was built at Wolverton for the North London on capital account and turned out of the works on 15 October 1910 (a similar train was also turned out the previous day).

The vehicles are either 30 feet or 28 feet long and 8 ft 6 in wide, and are gas-lit. From right to left their types and numbers are: Brake 3rd 101; 3rd 87; 1st 122; 1st 123; 2nd 122; 2nd 124; 1st 124; 3rd 88; 3rd 86; and Brake 3rd 102.

Birmingham & Sutton Set No 6, which was built on renewal account and turned out of the works on 24 March 1911. It seats 96 1st, 130 2nd and 276 3rd Class passengers. All vehicles are 30 feet long by 9 feet wide and are lit by oil gas. From right to left, their types and numbers are: Brake 3rd 7436; 3rd 7436; 3rd 639; 3rd 630; 3rd 628; 3rd 620; 1st 4583; 1st 4580; 1st 4548; 2nd 4897; 2nd 4894; Brake 2nd 6686. The 1sts are to D118, the 2nds and 3rds to D299, and the Brake ends to D362. The 2nds became 3rds in 1912, 4894/7 being renumbered 3241-2.

A view of two motor trains, each consisting of two 57-foot vehicles, built for the Longridge branch and photographed on completion at Wolverton in 1914. They were the only compartment-type motor train vehicles built new by the LNWR, all others being conversions. From right to left, they are: Driving Brake 3rd No 243, Composites Nos 3729 and 3728, and Driving Brake 3rd No 244.

It was suddenly discovered in 1915 that ordinary 9-foot-wide rolling-stock, which had been in use on the through Liverpool-Newcastle services for some time, actually fouled the North Eastern Railway loading gauge, and it had to be taken off the service! Consequently, in spite of wartime shortages of materials, two trains each of six carriages were specially built for it; they had recessed doors and handles to clear the NER loading gauge. This is Brake 3rd No 7471, 52 ft 6 in long by 9 feet wide, to D315A, on completion in 1917; it has exceptionally large luggage space. When these sets were demoted in LMS days, they were used on the Maryport & Carlisle section.

An end view of a high-roof corridor carriage, with the fuse box, electric light control switch, train alarm apparatus and other details well shown. The number '29' on the left indicates the weight of the coach in tons. These numbers began to be applied in 1914, and at about the same time the dimension plate was moved to the end; as it is not visible here, the date must be 1914. The letter 'R' indicates that the new (1913) pattern of steam-heat regulator is fitted. The reason for the chains and pulley apparatus is not known, but it is probably experimental - it is not to do with slipping apparatus as the vehicle is not a brake end.

*Right* A close-up view of the bogie of 50-foot by 8-foot Corridor Brake Composite No 1208, later 5943, of D216. The photograph was presumably taken because of the experimental fitting on the bogie frame, the purpose of which is not known.

*Below* A 57-foot underframe being lowered on to its bogies, which are the 1907 9-foot wheelbase deep-framed pattern; the date is about 1910.

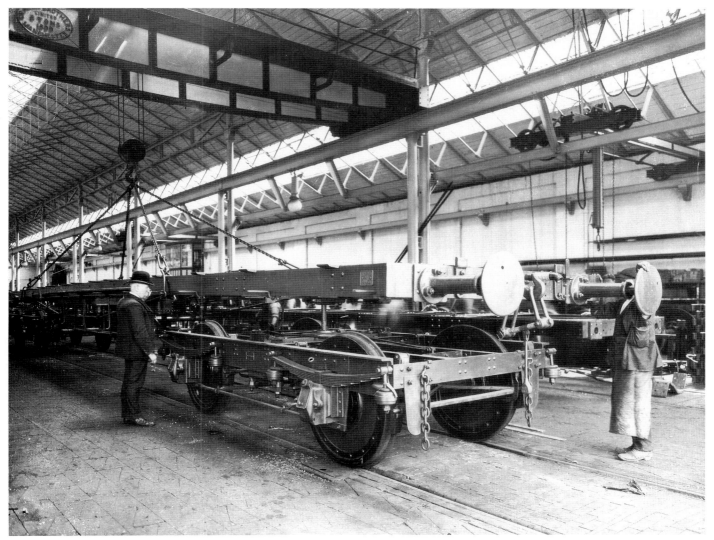

From time to time proposals were considered to combine old but serviceable vehicles together in various ways, so as to reduce deadweight. As early as 1907, a drawing was prepared for a 56-foot nine-compartment Composite, made up of a 28-foot 1st and 28-foot 3rd, but nothing came of it.

A scheme that was carried out, however, concerned the 28-foot four-wheelers built for the Broad Street-Mansion House 'Outer Circle' service in 1890-7 and for the Broad Street-Richmond service in 1910. The Richmond line was electrified on 1 October 1916, and surviving steam services were then cut back to operate between Willesden and Earls Court only and were worked by motor trains. Thus in 1917 90 redundant four-wheelers came to be loaned to the Government for service in France. One was destroyed there, but 89 returned, and all but one of them were reconstructed to make 44 56-foot

bogie vehicles between March 1920 and November 1921. Basically, two carriages were joined together on their existing underframes by means of a 3 ft 8 in piece of heavy angle iron, which was bolted across the joint in the solebars; it was partly concealed by the stepboard, which as usual at this period was in the high position, but the bolt heads at least can be seen in the photograph. New 8-foot-wheelbase bogies, of the 1916 design with 9-inch bulb-iron frames and wide hornplates were provided. The conversions produced 22 Brake 3rds, 11 3rds and 11 Composites, and they were made up into 11 trains of four carriages each for use on the Manchester (London Road) to Liverpool (Lime Street) services via Broadheath and Warrington (Low Level). As seen here, each train consisted of two Brake 3rds to D333B, one 3rd to D283A and one Composite to D176A or D176B. The Brake 3rd near the camera is No 7931; then comes 3rd No 1433.

Electric rolling-stock under construction at Wolverton about 1916 for the 'New Lines' between Euston and Watford.

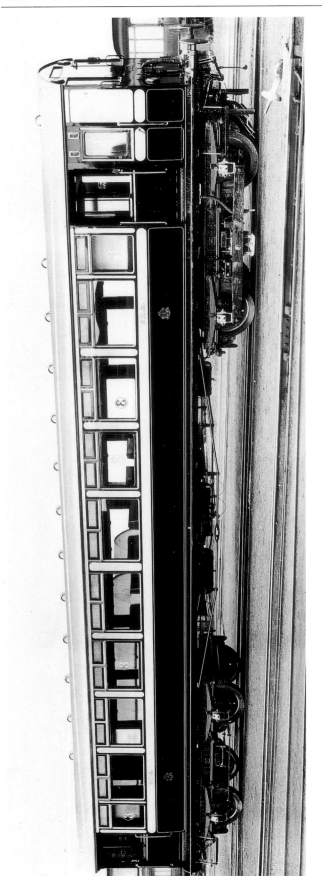

Electric 57-foot motor coach No 611E, with 3rd Class saloon, at Wolverton on completion about 1916.

Tube stock for the Bakerloo Line services to Watford, lettered 'L. & N. W. AND L. E. R.'.
The London Electric Railway took over the Piccadilly-Brompton, Charing Cross-Euston-Hampstead and Baker Street-Waterloo tube lines from 1 July 1910.

45-foot Open Scenery Truck No 12189 of D461B, built in 1920. It was one of three, all dual-fitted, which were equipped to take six luggage containers; they were lettered 'TO LOAD BETWEEN LONDON (EUSTON) AND DUBLIN (VIA) HOLYHEAD'. How long these containers remained in use is uncertain, but they are not believed to have survived after 1930.

Two more 45-foot Scenery Trucks were converted to carry four luggage containers for the London-Belfast service via Fleetwood, this one being No 12015. The containers are lettered 'L&Y AND L&NW JOINT RYS', so presumably the date is 1922.

'Claughton' No 30 *Thalaba* on an up Fleetwood Boat Express near Berkhamsted in 1924. The first vehicle is, of course, an open truck carrying luggage containers and the second is a picnic saloon.

# Ambulance trains

Quite early in the First World War ambulance trains were supplied by many railways to convey wounded personnel from the ports to hospitals throughout the country. They were all fitted with both vacuum and Westinghouse brakes and had to conform with the restricted loading gauge of the South Eastern & Chatham Railway. This view shows Home Ambulance Train No 7 as completed in 1914. The vehicles are, from left to right: 50-foot-long by 8-foot-wide arc-roof Brake 3rd No 7774 of D316; six Ward Cars converted from 45-foot clerestory-roof parcel sorting vans of D415 (the first one is No 9747); Dining Car No 5159, which was built as a kitchen dining saloon for the Euston-

Manchester service in 1890 (one of the first four LNWR vehicles built on bogies) and converted with centre gangways and gangways at the ends in 1897; and 42 feet by 8 ft 6 in Brake 3rd No 06568, built in 1884.

After the war the Ward Cars were converted to passenger brake vans to D381A and the Dining Car was reinstated but withdrawn before the Grouping, its body being sold for use as a holiday bungalow at Bognor. It has recently been rescued, however, and after restoration by Resco returned to service with the Great Scottish & Western Railway in Scotland in 1985.

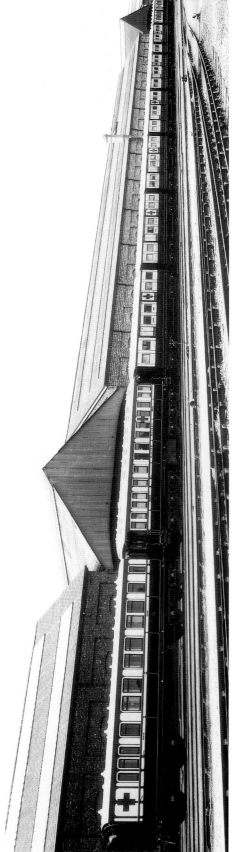

Home Ambulance Train No 8, also completed about October 1914, for the use of officers. The vehicles are, from left to right: No 5010, one of the rarely photographed 45 feet by 8 ft 6 in Family Saloons of D62, dating from 1894; No 5301, a 50 ft 6 in Dining Saloon, which was originally WCJS Kitchen Diner No 485, built in 1892, was

transferred to the LNWR in 1905, reinstated in traffic in October 1919 but withdrawn before the Grouping; six Ward Cars converted from parcel sorting vans to D415 (the first three being Nos 9762, 9751 and 9758); and 50 feet by 8 feet arc-roof Brake 3rd No 7672 of D316.

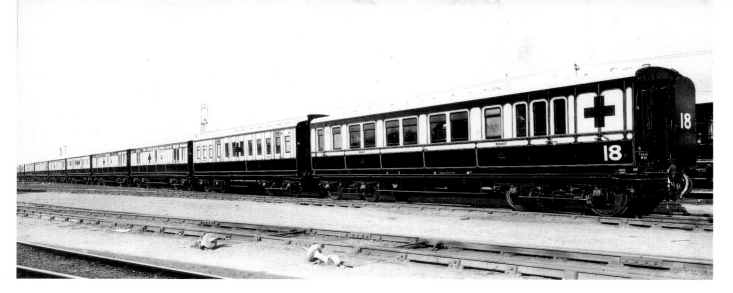

*Above* Home Ambulance Train No 18, which was completed on 8 March 1915. The vehicles are, from right to left: 45 feet by 8 ft 6 in Family Saloon No 5007 to D62, built in 1894; No 5160, one of the Manchester Diners, with a similar history to No 5159 opposite but a non-kitchen Diner; Ward Cars A and B; a Pharmacy Car converted from a 45-foot parcels van of D415; and three more Ward Cars, C-E. The Ward Cars are converted from Bicycle Vans of D430 dating from 1901. No 5160 was soon replaced by No 5303. All these vehicles were reinstated after the war, the Ward and Pharmacy Cars being converted to passenger brake vans.

*Below* Ambulance trains were also supplied for use on the Continent, and were all painted khaki. After the USA entered the war, many additional trains were ordered from several companies for use by the American troops. When the war ended, several were still under construction or had not yet been started; Wolverton had delivered 19 trains by the end of the war and 29 were under construction. This view shows part of US train No 56, which consisted of 16 vehicles, in the paintshop in September 1917. None of these carriages returned from the Continent after the war. They all have air brakes and side chains.

*Above* In 1884 four pairs of twin day saloons (each pair consisting of one ladies' saloon and one gentlemen's saloon) were built for the London-Liverpool/Manchester services. They were 42 feet long by 8 ft 6 in wide, and originally had radial underframes and arc roofs, each pair being connected by side gangways. In 1892 they were rebuilt with bogies of the 'truss-rod' type seen here and with cove roofs, and were thoroughly refitted to the best standards, after which they continued in use on the 'American Specials' for many years. Steam heating and gangways at the outer ends were fitted in 1897. The ladies' saloons were Nos 121-4 and the gentlemen's saloons 125-8, these numbers being increased by 5000 in the 1910 renumbering. The former ladies' saloons were altered to electric light about 1915, although the gentlemen's saloons seem to have remained gaslit. In 1919 Nos 5121 and 5122 were sold to the Government and converted to Pharmacy Cars for use in No 41 Continental Ambulance Train. This is one of these vehicles, in LNWR livery but

with WD number - the camouflage livery was not of course needed after the war. No 5121 later returned to the LNWR and was made into Service Car No 05121 of D8. As seen here, it is fitted with Spencer's heavy-duty buffers and side chains for use on the Continent. The oil axleboxes are the distinctive 1901 pattern.

*Below* During the war Wolverton built large numbers of horse-drawn vehicles for the forces. In November 1914, for example, an order was received for 850 vehicles; in fact, 200 had already been delivered and the balance was to be supplied at the rate of 50 a week, the cost of each one being £48 3s 5d. This view shows a train of these vehicles about to depart from Wolverton on the up slow line. The brake-van is No 1781B of D17A, lettered 'SWANSEA'; then come two wagons of D103, Nos 22581 and 2240, a deal wagon of D14 and two machinery trolleys of D38. All are loaded with general service waggons for the army.

# Lines around Northampton

A 'Superheated Goods Class G1', more commonly known simply as a 'Super D', leaving Northampton with a 60-wagon coal train for London on 9 July 1921. On the extreme right can be seen Northampton shed, the town itself forms the background to the train and on the extreme left, to the right of the church tower, can just be made out the signals controlling the south side of the station. The signal box in the centre is Duston Junction West, which was unusually arranged so that it could control both the main line, on which the train is running, and the line to Blisworth, which runs underneath the box. It is fully described in Jack Nelson's classic book, *LNWR Portrayed*. The distant signal, centre right, was fixed.

The engine is recorded as No 1487, which was built at Crewe in October 1918, but it seems likely that this number is incorrect, since the engine is fully lined, and lining ceased to be applied by Crewe Works paintshop on the outbreak of the First World War in September 1914. It was resumed from October 1921, but officially only for express passenger engines, although a few goods engines seem to have been done exceptionally. The tender is in plain black and is one of the type introduced by Bowen Cooke in 1916.

The train is made up very largely of private owner wagons from Staffordshire and Warwickshire collieries. So far as can be made out, from the engine backwards, they are: Gornall & Co of Brighton; two Kingsbury Collieries, the first of which is lettered 'Tamworth', if not the second; three Cannock & Leacroft Colliery; one Coggins & Arthur; one West Cannock; another Coggins & Arthur; a Faithfull; another West Cannock; a Foxfield, Blythe Bridge; an AGD; another West Cannock; an unidentifiable high-sided wagon; a Cannock Chase; a Bradfords; and then they generally become unidentifiable except for another Cannock Chase, an NSR wagon with the letters 'N' and 'S' either side of that company's 'Staffordshire knot' emblem, a Holly Bank and, well down the train, GER and LB&SCR wagons.

This splendid photograph has been published before, but is one of the finest ever taken of the traditional British goods train. Few who have ever heard a 'Super D' hard at work can fail to recreate in the mind's eye this summer evening scene and to imagine the sound for many minutes more as the engine accelerates its train up the gradient towards Roade.

*Above*  A very early view at Northampton (Castle) station, about 1876. The engine is a McConnell 0-4-2 goods engine that was built by the Southern Division at Wolverton in 1862, but has been modernised at Crewe with a Ramsbottom boiler, Webb chimney and other fittings. It is waiting with a ballast train - all the wagons have canvas flaps to prevent dust from getting into the axleboxes. The picture has clearly been posed, with all the men holding their positions for the camera. In the foreground beside the engine is George Webb, foreman platelayer, who came to Northampton in 1869 on a wage of 16 shillings a week. The post of the slotted signal is well utilised, supporting three arms.

*Above right*  A 'Greater Britain' Class three-cylinder compound, in quite immaculate condition, leaving Northampton with an up express in the late 1890s. The leading vehicle is a 32-foot Brake and the next one a 33-foot Composite. The latter had two lavatories, which were arranged in an unusual way, each one taking up a compartment across the full width of the body, instead of the more conventional arrangement, side by side with a diagonal partition.

*Right*  Another scene in Northampton (Castle) station as a 'Jumbo' attaches or detaches a horse-box at the rear of an up train. The left-hand signal is for the up through road to Bridge Street, the right-hand one for the up through to the main line.

*Above* The 12.25 pm seasonal excursion from Euston about to restart from Northampton on 10 August 1923. The engine, 'Claughton' No 207 *Sir Charles Cust*, has just taken water; the driver is climbing back into the cab after turning the water off and the fireman is about to climb down from the tender after taking the bag out and dropping it over the side. The train is in the extreme right-hand platform (looking at the picture), which was known as the 'riverside' platform, because when the station was rebuilt the river was diverted to run alongside it. From right to left, the signals are: down loop; down platform line; bay to down main; bay to down slow; down main platform to down main; and down main platform to down slow.

*Below* A 'Jumbo' leaving Northampton on a train to Market Harborough and Nottingham. The train consists of the following vehicles: a 42-foot Brake 3rd to D352; a 42-foot Composite to D163; another Brake 3rd to D352; and a 52 ft 6 in Corridor 3rd to D266. The Brake 3rds are both of the later pattern (the earlier vehicles had more windows in the van section and droplights in the luggage doors). They were built in 1893 for Liverpool-Leeds sets, most of which were transferred to the Crewe-Carlisle line about 1910 and were disbanded about 1920.

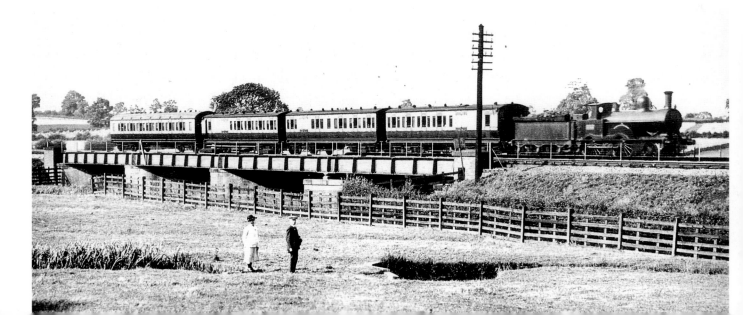

A view of Market Harborough station about 1859, taken from the down platform looking north-east.

Thrapston station, on the Northampton-Peterborough line, in the early 1920s, looking west. The goods train is carrying pig iron, which is en route to one of the ports, perhaps Liverpool, for loading into a ship as ballast.

# Rugby

*Above* An up Liverpool express leaves Rugby behind 'Prince of Wales' Class 4-6-0 No 1694 *Premier* and rebuilt 'Precursor' Class 4-4-0 No 412 *Marquis* about 1924. The first vehicle is an LNWR bullion van, the second an LYR carriage, and the rest of the train is a typically varied assortment of North Western stock. Bullion vans seem to have been conveyed regularly between Liverpool and Euston; a description of the vehicle was contained in the August 1906 issue of *The Railway Magazine*.

*Below* 'Prince of Wales' No 252 passes Clifton Road Junction, Rugby, with an up local passenger train. This was one of the 120 of the class built by William Beardmore & Co in 1921-2. They all had lamp irons from new, instead of LNWR sockets, and none were ever named.

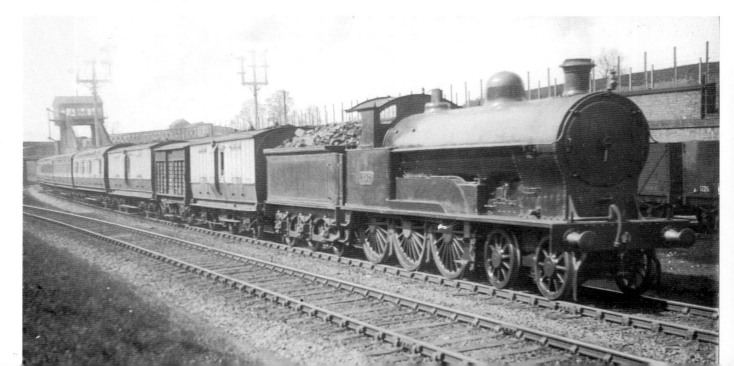

*Above* Rebuilt 'Precursor' No 688 *Hecate* leaves Rugby on an up express consisting of late-period 57-foot stock, probably in 1923. The engine is fitted with such late features as an oil box on the handrail, supplying pipes leading down inside the frames to the axleboxes, and a short horizontal handrail on the cab side.

*Right* 'Precursor' No 1516 *Alecto* passes beneath the Great Central girder bridge at Rugby with an up local passenger train about 1923. The locomotive is basically still in original condition, despite the oil box on the handrail, the short handrail on the cab side and the windshields on the sand-pipes, and was never in fact superheated. The prominent pipe leading from the cab across the top of the driving splasher and disappearing inside the frames connects the vacuum brake equipment in the cab with the crosshead vacuum pump, which was always positioned behind the right-hand cylinder on LNWR engines. The train is an arc-roof corridor set; two Corridor 3rds are in the centre, and the first and last vehicles are Brake 3rds to D317, conversions from centre Brake 3rds.

# Coventry area

*Left* Two views of Coventry station looking north. The first dates from about 1860, while in the second, later, view 'Large Bloomer' No 851 *Apollo* stands in the up platform with a Birmingham-Euston express. The date is difficult to determine precisely. The engine has been reboilered at Crewe and is in the early style of black livery, with the boiler bands fully lined. This style was changed in 1876, yet the engine also has a cab, which according to Ahrons was fitted in 1878 or 1879. In the centre road is a Ramsbottom 'DX' Class 0-6-0, which still seems to be in original condition with castellated chimney cap and painted numbers on the side-sheet, so would seem to be still painted green. On the other hand, it no longer has numbers on the front bufferbeam, which would seem therefore to be painted red. The 'Bloomer' was scrapped in 1881, so the date is probably the summer of 1879 or 1880. Although this is quite late for the 'DX' to be painted green (it was recorded in March 1880 that the last green engine had been painted black) and for the 'Bloomer' to have fully lined boiler bands, it is not impossible. The first vehicle of the express is a 21-foot four-wheeled van, a standard design of the 1860s. Next comes a Composite with central luggage compartment, dating from 1868.

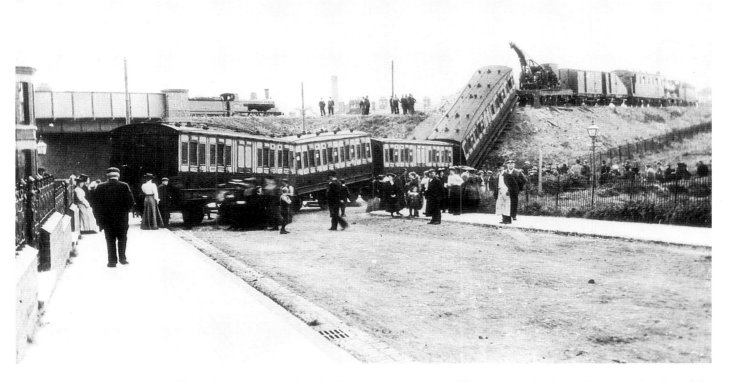

Albany Road, Coventry, in 1906, blocked by a rake of coaches that had become derailed while being marshalled for an excursion by the Swift Motor Company. They appear to be about to be returned to the rails by the way they had come! The bridge carries the Nuneaton branch.

Two views of the Daimler railcar, which was tried on the LNWR in 1918. It was kept at Daimler Halt, between Coventry and Nuneaton, and ran from Nuneaton to Rugby and Northampton via Market Harborough, returning to Rugby and Coventry via Kenilworth and Leamington. The first photograph was taken at Kenilworth, looking towards Leamington, and shows the railcar heading for Coventry. The second picture shows it en route, probably between Leamington and Rugby.

*Above* 'Cauliflower' 0-6-0 No 422, which was built in October 1900, at Hampton-in-Arden in July 1921. According to the records of the photographer, W. Leslie Good, the train is a 'Harwich Boat Express', but possibly there is an error as it appears to be an up local passenger, consisting of a 9-foot-wide Birmingham suburban set.

*Right* 'Prince of Wales' Class 4-6-0 No 1537 *Enchantress* passes Hampton-in-Arden with a Euston-Birmingham express in July 1921. *Enchantress* was one of the first batch of 'Princes', built in late 1911, which all had particularly fine names taken from ships of the Royal Navy; it appears to be still in original condition, with sandboxes beneath the running plate, oil boxes for the cylinders beneath the smokebox and the style of tender introduced for *Prince of Wales*.

# Birmingham

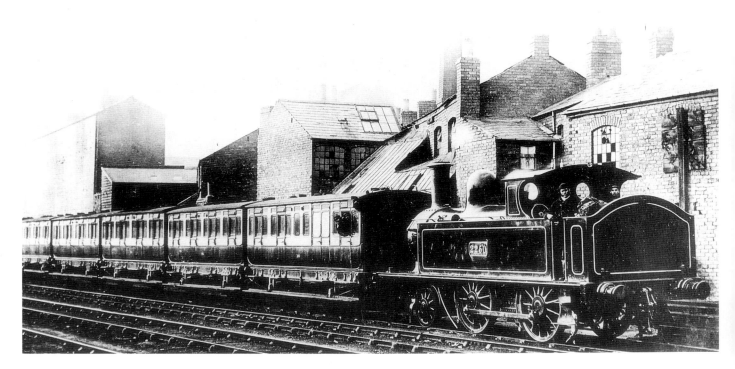

*Above*  A fairly well-known view but one of considerable interest, since it shows the type of suburban passenger train provided by the LNWR in the 1870s. At that time the major cities of England were growing rapidly, as new suburbs were built to accommodate the workers employed in the developing industries, and consequently suburban traffic as it is known today came into existence. The engine is Webb '4 ft 6 in 2-4-0' tank No 2250; it is in original condition with a cab as fitted to a tender engine, without rear spectacle plate, and carries a '10' shedplate, which was Aston. The four-wheel carriages date from the early 1860s and are all of about 24

feet in length (they were built to various lengths such as 23 ft 6 in and 22 ft 9 in). They still have individual footboards. The date is about 1878 and the location believed to be somewhere in the Birmingham area.

*Below*  Birmingham (New Street) station about 1885, seen from the west end looking east towards the footbridge, and showing the bridge-mounted signal cabin. The bridge leads to New Street on the left and to the bridge over Queen's Drive and to the Midland Railway side of the station on the right.

Another view of New Street in September 1885, taken at the top of the stairs leading from the New Street entrance on to the footbridge, and looking across the west end. The signalman in charge of the cabin on the bridge is watching operations intently. In platform 1 is 26 feet by 6 ft 10 in flat-sided Brake Van No 470, built in 1873; next to it is a 30 ft 6 in Composite.

A cast-iron notice at the entrance to Monument Lane shed, Birmingham. The photograph was taken in BR days on 14 December 1952, but the notice is of course original LNWR. In the LNWR list of steam sheds Monument Lane was shed 10M, a sub-shed of Aston, shed 10.

Two North Western railwaymen pose for the camera while relaxing on a typical LNWR station seat at Bescot in 1902.
On the left is a guard and on the right a porter.

# Lines around Nuneaton

An unidentified 'G' Class 0-8-0, the unsuperheated forerunner of the 'G1' Class, pulls out of Nuneaton up sidings with a heavy freight about 1910. It is one of the batch of 60 that was ordered by George Whale but built in 1910 after his retirement; they were virtually identical to the 'Piano Gs' converted from 'B' Class compound 0-8-0s, except that they did not have 'piano fronts'. The signal box has a canopy over certain windows, presumably to act as a protection from the glare of the sun and to keep the rain off if the signalman opened a window, for example to speak to a shunter. There is a bucket on the right-hand corner of the footboards round the box, so presumably the box 'lad' is cleaning the windows. Nuneaton Up Sidings was one of the company's hump yards and came into operation in about 1905; the hump itself is not in the picture, but is located on the far right and slightly behind the camera.

*Left*  A photograph taken from a down express at Nuneaton in 1901-3, looking across to what is probably a down Trent Valley line local, which is preparing for departure behind a 'Lady of the Lake' 2-2-2, probably from Stafford shed. The vehicle on the left is Composite No 889, which was built in May 1882 as a 32 feet by 7 ft 9 in Luggage 3rd, arranged 3rd, 3rd, luggage, 3rd, 3rd, and numbered 1478 in the 3rd Class series. In November 1900 it was altered to a Composite, basically by converting the luggage box to a compartment, and then had the unusual arrangement 3rd, 3rd, 2nd, 2nd, 2nd, as in this photograph. In May 1906 it became a 3rd, No 1859. It was supplemented in November 1911 as No 01859 and was withdrawn about 1915.

The second vehicle is Brake 2nd No 235, which was also built as a Luggage 3rd, No 513, in May 1881. In May 1900 it was extensively rebuilt as a one-compartment Brake 2nd, as here. Rebuildings like this were common practice on the LNWR and were done in a thorough and proper manner, so that the rebuilt vehicle looked just as if it had been so built in the first place. The central luggage doors seem to be 2 ft 6 in wide, instead of the usual 2 feet, though without a dividing moulding in the upper panel. The far end has been rebuilt to incorporate the usual 2 ft 6 in guard's ogee, but the side lamp is positioned at the end of the ogee and not centrally, an alteration made for new construction some 15 years earlier. No 235 was downgraded and supplemented in November 1909 as 3rd No 5064 and became 5064A at the renumbering; it was broken up in November 1915. These two carriages were part of Nuneaton, Shrewsbury and Liverpool Set No 1.

Next is a Cambrian Railways coach, a 21-foot horse-box and a 21-foot open fish truck, which is probably returning empty to South Wales via Shrewsbury and the Central Wales line. On the right a young lady seems to be saying goodbye to her fashionably dressed (!) mother on the platform. Above the former's head the communication cord can be clearly seen passing through the rings on the edge of the carriage roof.

*Below left*  A Nuneaton-Leicester train near Croft about 1910, hauled by '5 ft 6 in 2-4-2 Tank' No 2148. The first seven vehicles are a set of six-wheelers, mainly five-compartment 3rds. Then comes, perhaps, a 32-foot Composite; it is followed by a double-ended slip coach for Leicester, which has doubtless been slipped at Nuneaton from a down express.

*Above*  Glen Parva Junction signal cabin, part of the complex of junctions around Wigston, south of Leicester, about 1905. The stairs, door and foundation beam are brown, but everything above is buff with white window frames. On the wall on the left are three fire buckets with a mop on top, and beneath the stairs are probably oil drums, perhaps for signal and other lamps.

Two very early photographs taken at Hinckley, on the Nuneaton-Leicester branch, by E. Houlston about 1868. The first shows a McConnell 0-4-2 well tank, probably one of a batch of five built at Wolverton in 1860 with patent boilers and raised fireboxes. It perhaps has a Ramsbottom castellated chimney cap, though the chimney base seems original.

The second picture shows Sharp 2-2-2 saddle tank No 316, which was built originally as a 2-2-2 tender engine in the 1850s and obtained by the Birkenhead, Lancashire & Cheshire Junction Railway, on which it was No 21; it was acquired by the LNWR in November 1860 and worked largely on the Cromford & High Peak section before being rebuilt as a tank engine in April 1868; as it seems in ex-works condition, that might well be the date of the photograph. According to Alfred Rosling Bennett in *The Chronicles of Boulton's Siding*, the passenger service on this branch was worked wholly by Sharp 2-2-2 saddle tanks for 'a good portion of the 1870s'.

A puzzling feature of both pictures is that they show trains on what today would be considered the 'wrong line'. It has been suggested that the photographer's aim was to record the last working of the McConnell engine and the first of the Sharp rebuild.

# Tamworth and the Trent Valley line

*Above* Photographs at Tamworth after the First World War are quite common, but earlier ones are much more scarce. This busy scene at the south end of the station was taken in the late 1890s. A down express, double-headed by two compounds, a three-cylinder 'Dreadnought' and a four-cylinder 'Jubilee', heads north on the down fast line, while '5 ft 6 in 2-4-2 Tank' No 290 (probably of shed 14, Stafford) on a Trent Valley local takes water in the up platform.

*Below* Another view from the same period, poor technically but quite rare, since it shows a 'Greater Britain' Class three-cylinder compound passing Tamworth on a down express. The engine is No 527 *Henry Bessemer*.

*Above* 'Renown' Class 4-4-0 No 1929 *Polyphemus*, which was converted from a 'Jubilee' compound in February 1924, approaching Tamworth probably in the same year with an up Trent Valley local. The two outer carriages are ambulance conversions to D317, but the intermediate vehicles are a 42-foot Composite and a Luggage 3rd. Despite being a post-Grouping conversion, the engine is in pure LNWR condition, in plain black with no coat of arms, and is fitted with a 2,500-gallon Webb tender of the final type.

*Below and right* Three views of trains on the Trent Valley line in the late 1890s. The exact locations are uncertain, possibly because they are no longer recognisable due to quadrupling.

In the first (*below*) a sizeable down express is being double-headed by a 'Problem' and a 'Jumbo'; it is probably north of Lichfield on what seems to be a very windy day. The fireman of the 'Problem' has gone forward along the right-hand side of the engine to make some adjustments; perhaps the sand is not running freely from the sandbox.

The second photograph (*above right*) shows a 'DX' heading north on a down goods train somewhere on the same stretch of line. The white oval board at the top of the smokebox is obviously an indication of the class of train, but its exact meaning is unknown; other photographs of goods trains on this section show a white oval over the left-hand buffer.

Finally (*below right*) a '4 ft 6 in 2-4-2 Tank' heads an up Trent Valley local. It is thought to be either leaving Colwich or near Armitage (Rugeley-Colwich was quadrupled in 1903; Rugeley-Armitage on 29 March 1914). The first seven carriages are 30 ft 6 in long and date from the 1870s; the two end vehicles have been rebuilt as two-compartment Brake 3rds, and all have been reduced to four wheels, to save weight, and assembled as a close-coupled set for branch or suburban work. As such, the train is typical of stopping passenger trains at this period.

A view of the main line just south of Shugborough Tunnel from the up side looking north-west, showing damage done during a storm on 17 July 1918. The aqueduct in the foreground (which still exists today) no doubt added its contents to the flood when its abutment on the left was swept away. Clearly the only means of reopening the line was by shovel and sweat. The spot is little changed today, except for electrification masts and wires. Shugborough is the most northerly tunnel on the main line.

# Stafford area

A horse-dray loaded with blocks of ice and posed for the camera in South Street, Stafford, with St Thomas's Church school in the background. On the right is the LNWR carter and near the centre is Emanuele Giusso, an Italian ice-cream maker, who came to Stafford in 1902 and to whom the ice was consigned. Giusso regularly obtained supplies of ice from the Liverpool firm of H. T. Ropes, one of whose sales leaflets is also reproduced here.

ESTABLISHED 1844.

Telegrams: "ICEBERG," LIVERPOOL.
Telephone Bank 478.

## H. T. ROPES & CO., LTD.,
### Ice Merchants.

Offices:
34, NORTH JOHN STREET,
LIVERPOOL.

Stores:
72, 74, 76, Norfolk Street,
and
Rose Street, St. John's Fish Market.

Birkenhead Office and Stores:
95, CHESTER STREET.
Telephone 146 Birkenhead.

The Address has been the
same for

## 70 YEARS:

34, North John Street,
LIVERPOOL.

The Telegraphic Address is
"ICEBERG," LIVERPOOL.

The Telephone No. is
BANK 4743 LIVERPOOL
and
BIRKENHEAD 146.

### SOME — — — SUGGESTIONS

which, if borne in mind, may save many disappointments during the Summer Season, which is the only time that Ice may be a real want.

Owing to the curtailment of Postal Services it is almost useless to expect Ice to get away IF ORDERED BY LETTER POSTED ON THE DAY THE ICE SHOULD BE DESPATCHED FROM HERE.

Letters should be posted the Night previous at least.

If ordered by wire, orders must be in hand before noon.

The Goods Yards, and receiving Depots, close without warning at varying times during the day. All orders for despatch by goods trains should be in before noon all days.

All Goods Depots are entirely closed on each BANK HOLIDAY AND GOOD FRIDAY. ICE CANNOT THEREFORE BE SENT ON THOSE DAYS BY GOODS TRAIN.

If Ice is required by first trains it must be ordered the day previous. The first delivery of Letters is not received here till the first trains have gone.

Price is per Cash.

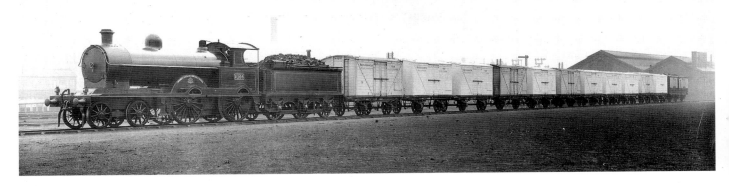

*Above* Ice would presumably be delivered in trains such as this rake of refrigerator vans to D46, which are all marked 'To Be Returned to Liverpool'. The first refrigerator vans on the LNWR were built in 1884, but the bulk of the construction took place in 1895-1902, by which time 558 were in service. The interior was kept cool by ice, which was loaded into compartments at the ends of each van through hatches in the roof; ladders up the ends gave access to the hatches. The engine is 'Precursor' Class 4-4-0 No 2166 *Shooting Star*, built in October 1905, the photograph having been taken between that year and 1910.

*Below* Webb 'Coal Tank' No 549 of shed 30 (Salop) in the Coalport bay at Wellington. The date must be about 1895, as the engine has a vacuum brake but is still in plain black livery. There was a rising gradient out of this platform and after the arrival of a train the stock was propelled out of the platform by the engine and allowed to run back in by gravity. This operation seems to have just been carried out. The stock is a four-coach close-coupled set of four-wheelers, which, from the board partly visible, appears to be 'SHREWSBURY AND WHITCHURCH No 1' set. The first and last vehicles are 27 ft 6 in by 7 ft 9 in 3rds. They were a common type, 202 being built with five compartments in 1871-2, but many were altered about 1890 to 1sts, 2nds, Composites and also 3rd Brake ends. They were supplemented in 1888-97 and broken up in 1898-1909. The second and third vehicles are (or, at least, were originally) Composites, and are 27 feet long by 8 feet wide. They were built in 1869-70 and were broken up in 1901-2. All the carriages retain their ogee-shaped headstocks. The fireman seems to find work on one of Mr Webb's 'basher tanks' enjoyable, despite the cramped footplate (a pricker is sticking out by the bunker handrail). All in all, a quite rare view of an early branch-line train.

*Above* Another 'Coal Tank', in lined black livery on a Pochin Collieries train of 20 coaches somewhere in South Wales. The first five vehicles are ancient LNWR carriages from the 1870s, 30 feet and 30 ft 6 in stock. All the carriages are in the brown livery used for workmen's trains; probably the reason why all the roofs are white is that they are covered with snow.

*Below* Rebuilt 'Precursor' Class 4-4-0 No 806 *Swiftsure* north of Stafford about 1925 with a down express, more likely a semi-fast, made up of 57-foot stock. The first carriage is a WCJS Corridor 3rd to D50, the second an LNWR Corridor 3rd to D264A, and then comes a four-coach non-corridor set.

An unidentified '6 ft 6 in Jumbo' on the last mile of the climb to Whitmore with the down 'Irish Day Express', 11 am from Euston, on 1 October 1900. The train is a very sizeable one of 13 vehicles. Leading is a six-wheeled brake van, then come three 50-foot corridors and a 12-wheeled dining saloon. In all the controversy over the compounds, it tends to be forgotten that the 'Jumbos' hauled loads such as this regularly and that there were 266 of them compared with 110 of the three-cylinder compounds. The fence at the top of the cutting behind the train had a number of boards in it that were used by Crewe Works for testing paint.

An unidentified 'DX' 0-6-0 passes Madeley on the up fast line about 1890. Perhaps the train is empty stock, as the engine is not fitted to operate the continuous brake or communication cord. The stock is: a 19-foot covered carriage truck with high arc roof; three horse-boxes, 19 ft 6 in, 16 feet and 19 ft 6 in long respectively; a 21-foot combination truck; two 19-foot covered carriage trucks, one with a high roof and the other with a low arc roof of 1872; two 32-foot five-compartment parcel vans; a 19-foot covered carriage truck; two parcel sorting vans, a 30 ft 1 in and a 32-footer; a 30 ft 6 in full brake; a 30 ft 1 in parcel sorting van; a 16-foot open carriage truck; an unidentified four-wheeled vehicle; and a four-coach set of 30-foot or 30 ft 6 in vehicles.

The signal box is of unusual design, the corner nearest the camera being greater than a right-angle, for some reason not known. Beyond the box is the engine shed of the Lycett Colliery Company. In the foreground, the down slow line is still laid with 21-foot rail, the other three tracks having 30-foot.

Two views of Betley Road station taken one winter in the 1890s. Both are taken looking south, the first along the up fast line, the second along the down slow line. The building on the right is probably the original station building, erected by the Grand Junction Railway, and the one on the left is a later LNWR building. The Stafford-Crewe section was quadrupled in 1876. Before then, according to G. P. Neele, there had been queues of trains waiting for a chance to work northwards, but the widening merely transferred these 'blockades' of trains to Crewe, which was often in a 'chronic state of block'!

# The Royal Train

Saloon in 1879 and later became a Sleeping Saloon but was not included in any diagram book; it was supplemented in May 1905 and withdrawn in November 1913); two 32-foot Day Saloons; 42-foot Saloon No 153; 32-foot Family Saloon No 63; 32-foot Sleeping Saloon No 1 or No 65; Queen Victoria's Saloon (now joined on one underframe); and 42-foot Saloon No 131 (for equerries).

*Below* The two six-wheeled Saloons built to the design of Richard Bore at Wolverton in 1869 for Queen Victoria, photographed here in October 1888, possibly after being fitted with automatic vacuum brake - the pipes linking them seem to indicate they actually have both vacuum and Westinghouse brakes. They are oil-lit and were the first carriages in the country to be connected by a gangway enclosed in flexible bellows. The livery is indeed lavish; the panelling on the upper body is complemented by similar 'panelling' on the underframes, and the same light colour also appears on the spring blocks and axleboxes; gilded crowns and similar devices adorn the underframes and body sides, and the ends of the headstocks are carved with lion heads, while between the edge of the roof and the top of the body panelling is what appears to be an oak-leaf border; the Royal Arms are displayed in the centre of the body sides with Queen Victoria's arms on either side. These saloons were rebuilt on one 12-wheeled underframe in 1895.

*Top* The Royal Train photographed in 1888-9. The engine, 'Dreadnought' Class three-cylinder compound 2-2-2-0 No 410 *City of Liverpool*, is in original condition. The location is uncertain, but is thought to be somewhere on the descent from Whitmore to Crewe, probably near Basford sand sidings. The leading vehicles of the train consist of: 32-foot Brake Van No 210; 32-foot 1st No 75 (for LNWR officials); 27-foot Saloon No 4 (which carried LNWR directors and was built in 1864 as a Royal Sleeping Saloon; it later became Mr Park's Saloon, then Mr Earl's Saloon and subsequently became Family Saloon No 2004A, being broken up in March 1920); 42-foot Saloon No 153 (built in 1888); 32-foot Sleeping Carriage No 1 (built in 1879); twin Queen Victoria Saloons; 32-foot Family Saloon No 63 (for the Queen's maids; built in 1875); 32-foot Sleeping Carriage No 65 (built in 1875); a 32-foot Family Saloon; then two unidentified vehicles, followed by 33-foot Lavatory Composite No 999; and 32-foot Brake Van No 272.

*Above* The Royal Train on 25 May 1897, hauled by 'Greater Britain' Class three-cylinder compound 2-2-2-2 No 2053 *Greater Britain* in the special scarlet livery that it carried in honour of Queen Victoria's Diamond Jubilee. Again the location is not certain, but is thought to be Wolverton. The train consists of 32-foot Brake Van No 210; 32-foot Sleeping Saloon No 132 (an exceptional vehicle, which was built as a Royal

*Above*  An interior view of the Prince of Wales's Saloon about 1888.

*Above right*  Looking south at Wrinehill, on the main line south of Crewe, the pilot engine of the Royal Train passes on the down fast line, in front of a fair crowd of spectators watching over the fence on the right. The engine is an immaculate 'Lady of the Lake' 2-2-2 and the date some time in the early 1890s. The procedure was for the pilot engine to precede the Royal Train by 15 minutes; no other train was allowed to follow the Royal Train until a further 15 minutes had elapsed after its departure. In the middle distance on the right can be seen a platelayer, following the long-established practice that plate-layers lined the route of the Royal Train. In September 1910 the Chief Engineer replied to a request from the Chairman for information about the date when the special precautions for the working of the Royal Train were brought into use. In reply he sent a copy of a notice issued by the Northern Division Head Office at Stafford on 1 September 1853. It gave the timings of a journey by the Royal Train from Chester to Scotland on 5 September and continued:

'All Platelayers are to cease working on the line (except in case of emergency) at 9 am and act as Policemen until the train has passed a quarter of an hour. They will patrol the line in their respective lengths and are to be careful not to allow any Horses or Cattle to cross the line for a full half-hour before the train is due. Should anything go wrong they are required to give timely notice to the driver of the train.

'The leading man of each gang must be on duty at every crossing and siding where there is no policeman and must on no account allow any Engine or Train to be upon the Down line for full three-quarters of an hour before the Royal Train is due.

'No Ballast Engine or Wagon must be allowed upon the line at any point for the same period.'

*Right*  Another Royal Train pilot, this time 'Jumbo' No 861 *Amazon*, probably on the up fast line somewhere just south of Crewe on 8 October 1921. The single carriage presumably conveys staff and officials.

The Royal Train hauled by two 'Alfred the Great' Class 4-4-0s, emerging from Whitmore cutting on the up fast line on 15 May 1904; they have completed the climb from Crewe and have begun the descent towards Stafford. The first vehicle is one of the two Royal Train Brake Vans, either No 73 or 86, and the second vehicle is a 45-foot Family Saloon to D63. In 1904 the Brake Vans were rebuilt with clerestory roofs to match the rest of the train.

The scene at Euston in October 1926 when nine retired Crewe drivers were presented to King George V and Queen Mary on the arrival of the Royal Train from Scotland. The nine men were Alfred Eachus, William Jeffries, William Hughes, Samuel Galley, J. Tansley Hollins, John Ford, John Jones, Sampson Wright and Wilfred Elson. All were over 70 years of age and had over 50 years of railway service. Between them they had driven the Royal Train for almost 20,000 miles. The *Crewe Chronicle* reported the occasion at length on 15 October and referred to the men as 'knights of the footplate', 'men of unimpeachable character' and the 'finest type of engine driver in the country'.

# Crewe

An unidentified 'Jumbo' leaves Crewe on an up express. In fact, it seems to have stopped just south of the junction with the North Staffordshire Railway line to Stoke-on-Trent for the photograph to be taken, as the guard and several passengers are leaning out watching the photographer. The leading vehicles are a flat-sided brake van dating from the early 1870s, a luggage composite from the same period that seems rather tired, being down at the far end, a 30 ft 1 in five-compartment 3rd, a 26-foot brake van converted to a milk van, another 30 ft 1 in five-compartment 3rd, and a 32-foot composite.

Another view at the same location but looking in the opposite direction, as the 2 pm 'Corridor' approaches behind an 'Alfred the Great' Class 4-4-0 on 3 April 1903. On the left is the North Staffordshire line to Stoke-on-Trent, with slotted signals and engine shed prominent; on the right is a three-cylinder compound 0-8-0, waiting for the road through the station. The goods lines have clearly been 'kinked' to make way for the signal gantry. At this time all trains, goods as well as passenger, still passed through the station, the goods avoiding lines under the north junction not yet having been completed.

*Left* At first glance a quite unremarkable picture, but closer examination shows it to be quite rare. The engine is No 1501 *Iron Duke* in original condition with a double chimney and working as a four-cylinder simple. As such, it had no lubricator on the running plate above the outside cylinders, and this is one of the very few photographs showing it in this condition. It is standing in the main up platform at Crewe.

*Below left* 'Greater Britain' Class three-cylinder compound 2-2-2-2 No 2052 *Prince George* leaving Crewe in the late 1890s with a down express; it is in the superb condition typical of the time. The leading vehicle is a 32-foot Luggage Composite; it is followed by one of the original WCJS 32-foot Sleeping Composites, which were built in 1876-8, transferred to the LNWR in 1899 and withdrawn some ten years later. The 'spider bridge' (see overleaf) is on the right, while on the left are three wagons of the Madeley Coal & Iron Co. Beyond them is the Crewe Arms Hotel, and on the extreme left is a splendid lamp, somewhat out of focus. On the water column is a box, into which drivers of 'foreign' engines (that is, engines of other companies such as the Great Western and North Staffordshire) who took water at the column, had to place a ticket recording the fact, so that their company could be charged later.

*Right* A notice on a water column at Crewe instructing 'foreign' drivers to put a water ticket in the box.

*Below* 'Jubilee' Class four-cylinder compound No 1910 *Cavalier*, in almost exactly the same position as *Prince George*, on 14 May 1901. The first vehicle is a 30 ft 1 in 3rd; it is followed by a vehicle of some rarity, a 32 feet by 7 ft 9 in Composite, with compartments: ½ 1st, 3rd, 2nd, 1st, ½ 1st. About 23 of these carriages were built in 1876-9, and were bow-ended. They were supplemented between 1899 and 1906 and were broken up between 1907 and 1915. The third vehicle is a 42-foot centre brake radial 3rd to D354.

This and the photograph opposite were taken before Crewe station was enlarged and burrowing junctions constructed at the north

end. The alterations were approved in 1896 but were not completed until 1906. After the 1985 alterations, Crewe station has basically reverted to this layout, with two island platforms. The Crewe Arms still stands.

A view looking north-west from the west end of the footbridge that linked all the platforms, near the ramp leading down to the North shed, taken a few months after the Grouping (there is a 30 ft 1 in van in LMS lake in the background). A 'Prince of Wales' Class 4-6-0, un-named but clean and in plain black paint, is heading north on a down express. After passing under the 'spider bridge' it will swing to the left behind the North Junction signal box and head down the main line.

The 'spider bridge' linked the Works with the station, carrying an extension of the Works internal narrow gauge railway and enabling parts to be dispatched quickly by passenger train to any part of the LNWR system. As can be seen, the track actually passed through the signal box at the North Junction.

It is a pity that the photograph is slightly blurred and that the carriage numbers are illegible. Behind the engine is a 57-foot five-compartment Corridor Brake 3rd to D307 dating from 1907 and built with the 'toplight' style of body framing. Next

comes a 52 ft 6 in Corridor Composite to D136 dating from 1911; these vehicles were tri-composites until the abolition of 2nd Class and were gas-lit at first, although this one has already been converted to electricity on the Wolverton system. Next comes another 'toplight', a 57-foot double-ended Corridor Brake Composite to D206, of which seven examples were built. According to the roof boards, these three vehicles form a through portion from London (Euston) to an undecipherable destination, which looks like Prestatyn, but as the train is heading down the Warrington line is possibly Barrow or Keswick. The fourth vehicle is a cove-roof Brake end, perhaps to D310.

Perhaps the most interesting vehicles are in the background. Prominent are two Red Wharf Bay branch saloons, Nos 5079 and 5078, while in the far background is a Brake Van to D375 with pure white roof, evidence that repaired as well as new carriages had their roofs painted white.

*Above* Looking north off the main up platform, No 5, on the same occasion. The footbridge linking the north ends of all the platforms and, at its extremity out of the picture on the left, the North shed, is prominent. In the distance, on the right, is the signal gantry across the main line to Carlisle and Liverpool, while on the left, beyond the 'spider bridge', two 'Claughtons' await their next turns of duty.

*Below* 'Precursor' No 1297 *Phalaris* on Crewe North shed, with No 1115 *Apollo* and another of the class alongside, probably about 1907. The pipe down the chimney of *Phalaris* appears to be to provide steam to act as a draught on the fire, before the engine's own boiler has raised enough pressure to operate the blower.

# War memorials

The war memorial inside the steam shed at Chester, shed 19, probably soon after erection in the early 1920s. Similar memorials were erected at several sheds, known examples being at Crewe and Rugby, where Remembrance services were held for many years on Armistice Day. What generally became of these memorials when the sheds were demolished is not known, but the one at Rugby was re-erected in the BR electric traction depot.

Rugby Railway Band, which played at the annual Armistice Day service at Rugby, posed beside 'Claughton' *L/Corpl J. A. Christie* VC in November 1927. Sitting on the front row, left to right, are: F. House (S&T linesman); W. Jones (driver); G. W. Walton (retired MPD Superintendent); Capt R. F. Harvey (District Superintendent, Rugby MPD); P. O'Malley (President, and owner of 'O'Malley's', a public house in Rugby where the band practised and which still exists today); A. Isham (bandmaster); Mr Fox (Station Master, Rugby Central); J. Mottram (S&T Superintendent); T. Clay (Secretary; driver); W. Hill; and T. Townsend.

Centre row, standing: T. Sheffield (driver); R. Hutt; A. Reece; E. Welch (fitter); S. Folwell (steam raiser); L. Clarke; A. Walker; J. Johnson; A. Broome; L. Liggins; Skellern; W. Ashby; R. Loader; E. Harris; B. Loader; and G. Townsend (standing; retired).

Back row: K. Loader; J. Wheatley; C. H. Lee (coppersmith; he became deputy bandmaster and in 1974 was made a Commander of the Order of St John in recognition of his work for the railway first aid movement); E. Coles (driver); P. Baseley; R. Pettifer; H. Gardner (PW Department); J. W. Lee; H. Lane; and F. Spreadbury (engineers dept).

All members were either railwaymen or relatives of in-service railwaymen.

'Prince of Wales' No 2275 *Edith Cavell*, decorated with wreaths for the Armistice Service at Crewe North shed. This engine was named after the celebrated British nurse who was working at a hospital in Brussels and who was shot by the Germans for helping British soldiers to escape to Holland.

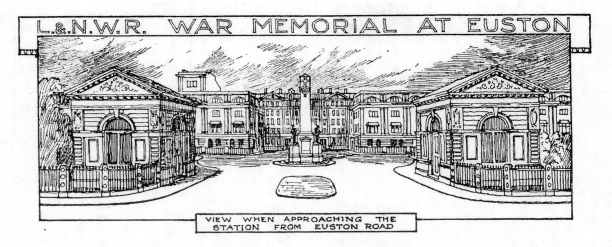

**L.&.N.W.R. WAR MEMORIAL AT EUSTON**

VIEW WHEN APPROACHING THE
STATION FROM EUSTON ROAD

London and North Western Railway,
Euston Station.
October, 1919.

PROPOSED WAR MEMORIAL.

In the Great War 3,649 London and North Western Railwaymen laid down their lives for their Country and the Cause of Right.

Their fellow workers no doubt desire that some permanent memorial should be erected to commemorate this splendid loyalty and devotion to duty.

A Committee, composed of some of the Company's Directors, Officers and Men, have been looking into this matter, and they recommend that a suitable monument be erected on the most prominent site available, viz., Euston Square, as shown on the sketch at the top of this sheet. This Memorial would be seen by the millions of travellers from all parts of the world who pass along Euston Road or use our Railway.

The Committee feel sure that all members of the staff will desire to associate themselves with this Memorial to their fellow workers, and will welcome the opportunity of contributing to its cost. This it is estimated will amount to about £10,000. The Company would bear the whole cost of the necessary road alterations, &c.

It is suggested that a minimum amount of 2s. 6d. be subscribed by anyone desiring to associate themselves with this Memorial, and should you wish to do this, please fill in the attached perforated slip and hand it to the person from whom you received it.

It is the intention of the Company to present to the relatives of those London and North Western Railwaymen who died a suitably decorated Memorial Album, showing the names of all who laid down their lives, also of those who received Military Honours, together with a page giving some particulars of the work done by those who stayed at home.

The book will also be for sale at net cost price to any London and North Western employee.

*G H Claughton*
Chairman

After the First World War, this circular letter was sent by the Chairman, Sir Gilbert Claughton, to all employees of the company asking for contributions to erect a memorial to those of their fellows who had lost their lives. The war memorial was eventually erected at Euston to the design depicted in the letter heading, and still exists today; the 'Memorial Album' was also produced, but was entitled The Roll of Honour.

# Lines to Derby

*Above* 'Renown' Class 4-4-0 No 1958 *Royal Oak* runs through Pear Tree & Normanton on the Midland Railway with an express heading for Derby. The train consists of one LNWR carriage, a 50-foot 3rd, and a five-coach North Staffordshire Railway set. Probably the date is mid-1922, as the engine was rebuilt from an 'Alfred the Great' in April 1922 and it still seems very clean, in the full lined livery and in unaltered LNWR condition.

*Below* A passenger train for Walsall leaving Derby in early LMS days behind 'Cauliflower' No 577. The engine was fitted with a Belpaire firebox in 1924 and was scrapped in 1927; the train is a 57-foot non-corridor set, made up of Brake 3rds to D333 front and rear, a Composite to D176 and a 3rd to D283.

'George the Fifth' Class 4-4-0 No 882 *Canada* leaving Derby on a passenger train for Crewe about 1925. It has a Belpaire firebox, and the sides of the cab roof have been cut back to suit the LMS composite loading gauge, but otherwise its condition is pure LNWR. The first vehicle is a 30-foot fruit van to D454, one of 25 built in 1909 and converted to fish vans in 1921-2 for Milford Haven traffic; the second vehicle is perhaps North Staffordshire; then comes a 50-foot cove-roof set, 9 feet wide, which was originally a Birmingham-Manchester set but by this time has become an Inter-District set.

# The North Wales line

Technically a poor picture, but one of some interest, since it is thought to be the only photograph showing a Webb 'Precursor' Class 2-4-0 on a train. The location is believed to be Saltney Junction, west of Chester, where the GWR line to Wrexham and Shrewsbury diverges from the LNWR main line to Holyhead. If this is so, the train is, of course, on the main line.

An unidentified 'Precursor' passing Colwyn Bay about 1908 with the up day 'Irish Mail'. The load is difficult to determine precisely, as the rear of the train is obscured by steam, but it is certainly substantial. Although the 'Georges' and 'Princes' came to be used on these trains later, 'Claughtons' did not work to Holyhead in LNWR days, as the turntable there was not long enough to take them. It was not until the late 1920s that a large turntable was installed to take 'Royal Scots' as well as 'Claughtons'.

Ramsbottom 'DX' Class 0-6-0 No 1974 at Colwyn Bay, probably in the early 1890s. It was built as No 1316 in May 1864, renumbered 1974 on the duplicate list in December 1890 and scrapped in December 1900. Photographs of 'DXs' numbered in the 1800 series duplicate list are quite rare, the 3000 series list being introduced in 1897. The engine has a white oval board in the socket over the left-hand buffer and is on a ballast train, the letter 'N' of 'NWD' (North Wales Division) being just visible on the end of the front wagon.

*Above* The up day 'Irish Mail' about to leave Holyhead for Euston in July 1898. It is double-headed by 'Problem' Class 2-2-2 No 61 *Phosphorus* and a Webb three-cylinder compound, either an 'Experiment' or, more probably, a 'Dreadnought'. The Holyhead expresses were often double-headed by some such combination as this, as indeed was any sizeable LNWR express at this period. The 'Problem' is unusual in that although in its final form as rebuilt by Webb, it has a 1,500-gallon tender without coal rails. As a general rule, the rebuilt engines had 1,800-gallon tenders with coal rails. On the extreme left is a mobile water tank for topping up carriage supplies.

*Below* Another view of an express about to leave Holyhead. Again, the pilot is a 'Problem', but the train engine is a 'Jubilee' four-cylinder compound 4-4-0 with a capuchon on the chimney, which dates the picture at about 1903.

This picture, or rather a slightly different one taken on the same occasion, has appeared in a previous book, but it seems well worth using here, since a print from the original glass negative has become available, enabling far superior reproduction to be achieved. It shows the Royal Train awaiting departure from Holyhead about 1900. The engine is 'Jubilee' Class four-cylinder compound 4-4-0 No 1916 *Implacable*. It has the commu-nication cord rigged to the train. The leading vehicle is Brake Van No 272 and the sec-ond is Queen Victoria's fourgon truck No 100 (later 11100), which became LMS No 4039 and was scrapped in 1934. It was turned out of Wolverton Works on 13 May 1898 and was in effect a special enclosed carriage truck; the Royal carriage had previ-ously been carried on an ordinary open carriage truck.

A general view of the Holyhead Hotel and station from the harbour side.

A close-up view of the clock tower commemorating the opening of the extension to the harbour by the Prince of Wales on 17 June 1880.

# The 'American Specials'

*Above*  A down 'American Special' on the main line just north of Crewe station, hauled by a '6 ft 6 in Jumbo' in 1898-9. The first vehicle is a 32-foot Brake Van, then comes a 42 feet by 8 ft 6 in Radial Saloon built in 1884 for the purpose seen here, to run next to a Dining Saloon, in this case a 50 ft 6 in WCJS example; a 65 ft 6 in Dining Saloon to D30, which is new; a 5½-compartment 45-foot WCJS Corridor Composite to D31; a pair of Saloons, one for gentlemen, the other for ladies; perhaps another WCJS vehicle; and a Brake Van.

*Below*  Inside Liverpool Riverside station, two 'Special Tanks' have brought in an 'American Special' for Euston, which now waits for its passengers to transfer from their Atlantic liner. The nearest carriage appears to be one of the rare Corridor Brake 3rds of D127. Another 'Special Tank' is standing in the far platform, probably with another 'American Special'.

Riverside Railway Station. LIVERPOOL.

*Above* At the inner end of Liverpool (Riverside) station two 'Special Tanks' have brought in an 'American Special' for Euston on 3 August 1904. The engine furthest from the camera is an ordinary member of the class, albeit one with a cab, but the near-er one seems to be *Euston*, one of the two engines fitted with square tanks and condensing apparatus for working through the Liverpool tunnels. On the left is part of 45-foot Brake Van No 70 of D381, built in 1900. It is one of the later batches with bulb-iron frames and square headstocks, and with the ogees directly opposite each other, as opposed to the previous batches in which they were diagonally opposite. The rain strip on the roof is quite prominent and communication-cord rings are fitted, despite the late date of construction. The letters 'L&NWR' were not dis-played on the waist panels of coaching stock except on brake vans with central ogees.

*Below* A little further along the same train. On the left is Dining Saloon No 198, one of three vehicles, Nos 196-8, built to D30 in 1897; they were the first 65 ft 6 in long vehicles. Next to it is one of the original 42-foot Brake 3rds, 8 ft 6 in wide, built in 1884 and rebuilt in 1898 with corridors and with the outer-end compart-ments converted into lavatories.

*Right* Another view of Dining Saloon No 198, awaiting departure from Euston about 1900.

*Below* A third view of the same train, but still further along the platform. On the left is Saloon No 127, which was built in 1884 as a gentlemen's day saloon and was partnered with ladies' saloon No 124 as a twin set. They had arc roofs and side gangways, and were radial. In 1892 they were rebuilt with bogies and cove roofs. They were some of the earliest vehicles to be fitted with steam heating, in 1897, and with central gangways at both ends. No 127 became 5127 in the 1910 renumbering and is D53 in the 1915 Diagram Book where it is shown as still gas-lit.

Beyond it is 34-foot Dining Saloon No 118, which was one of a pair of day saloons built in 1883 and converted to a dining saloon in 1889, its original six-wheel underframe being replaced by a bogie underframe. This and all the other day saloons of this type built for the Liverpool boat trains in 1882-5 must have proved unsatisfactory for some reason, since in 1896 it was proposed to convert them into picnic saloons; perhaps they rode badly. They were supplemented in 1898 and were withdrawn in 1904. The one exception was No 118, which was converted to a kitchen car and remained in service, doubtless on the Liverpool boat trains, until after the First World War. It became 2118 in the 1910 renumbering. In April 1916 (restaurant cars were withdrawn in that year) it was converted for use in Naval Ambulance Train No 4 and was noted as 'Not For Repairs' when this train was taken into Wolverton Works in November 1919.

*Above* Two 'Special Tanks', Nos 28 and 1614, await the 'right away' from Liverpool (Riverside) with an up 'American Special' about 1910. At Edge Hill they will of course be replaced by the main-line engine.

*Below* Carriages waiting for trade outside Riverside station. The three on the left all appear to belong to the White Star Line, which company began to use Southampton in June 1907, Cunard following in 1920.

The purpose of the 'American Specials' was to convey passengers between London and the transatlantic liners at Liverpool. Here the White Star liner *Oceanic* embarks passengers for New York at Prince's Stage, Liverpool. Presumably she will call at Queenstown (now Cobh) in Southern Ireland, as the sacks of mail on the barrows by the gangway are labelled to destinations such as Winnipeg, Boston and Chicago via Queenstown. The LNWR had offices and agents in several American cities and its links with the other side of the Atlantic were recognised in the names of its engines. 'Dreadnoughts' were named *City of New York* and *City of Chicago* in the mid-1880s and, with one exception, the names of the 'Teutonics' were inspired by White Star liners, whose names ended in '-ic', No 1302 being *Oceanic*.

VIII

# London and North Western Railway.

# AMERICA
## VIA LIVERPOOL.

The Special Trains run between LIVERPOOL and LONDON by the London and North Western Railway Company for American travellers arrive at, and depart from, the

### RIVERSIDE STATION at LIVERPOOL,

adjoining the Landing Stage, at which the Atlantic Steamers are berthed.

Baggage of Passengers arriving from America, directly it passes through the Custom House, is placed in the Train, which is standing alongside the Custom House; and both for incoming and outgoing travellers the expense and inconvenience of crossing the City of Liverpool are entirely avoided.

During the month of September, AMERICAN SPECIALS with Luncheon Cars attached leave EUSTON STATION, LONDON, for the RIVERSIDE STATION, in LIVERPOOL, as follows:—

| | Steamer. | | Steamer. |
|---|---|---|---|
| Tuesday, September 1st—12 o noon..."Servia." | | Wednesday, Sept. 16th—12 30 noon..."Germanic" | |
| Wednesday, „ 2nd—12 30 noon..."Britannic." | | | {"Catalonia." |
| Thursday, „ 3rd—12 o noon | {"Bothnia." | Thursday, „ 17th—12 o noon | {"Labrador." |
| | {*"Scotsman" | | {*"Numidian." |
| | {*"Mongolian" | Saturday, „ 19th—12 o noon..."Etruria." | |
| Saturday, „ 5th—12 o noon..."Umbria." | | Wednesday, „ 23rd—12 30 noon..."Teutonic." | |
| Wednesday, „ 9th—12 30 noon..."Majestic." | | Thursday, „ 24th—12 o noon | {"Cephalonia." |
| Thursday, „ 10th—12 o noon | {"Pavonia." | | {"Parisian." |
| | {"Sardinian." | Saturday, „ 26th—10 55 a.m...."Campania." | |
| Saturday, „ 12th—12 o noon..."Lucania." | | Wednesday, „ 30th—12 30 noon..."Britannic." | |
| Tuesday, „ 15th—12 o noon..."Aurania." | | | |

*—A separate portion for Alexandra Dock will be attached to the Riverside Special, leaving London (Euston Station) at 12.0 noon, on the 3rd and 17th September, for Passengers embarking by these Steamers, **which leave** from **the Alexandra Dock** and **not** from the Landing Stage.

## MAIL SERVICES (via Dublin & Queenstown) with AMERICA.

Passengers (First and Second Class) joining or leaving the Atlantic Steamers at Queenstown can avail themselves of the following Services via Holyhead and Dublin:—

| TO AMERICA. | Wednesdays. | Saturdays. | FROM AMERICA. | Week-days. |
|---|---|---|---|---|
| London (Euston) ............depart | 8 20 p.m. | 4 10 p.m. | | |
| Birmingham (New St.)... „ | 10 15 „ | 5 50 „ | | |
| Bristol (via Severn T'nel) „ | 7 40 „ | 12 30 noon | Queenstown ...............depart | 2 10 p.m. |
| „ (via Birmingham) „ | 7 0 „ | 3 15 p.m. | Kingstown (Pier).......{arrive | 7 15 „ |
| Chester ........................ „ | 12 38 a.m. | 8 25 „ | {depart | 7 25 „ |
| Edinburgh (Princes St.) „ | 6 0 p.m. | 2 0 „ | Holyhead (Pier)............ „ | 11 45 „ |
| Glasgow (Central)......... „ | 5 55 „ | 2 0 „ | Manchester (Exchange)arrive | 3 55 a.m. |
| Liverpool (Lime Street)... „ | 11 10 „ | 7 15 „ | Liverpool (Lime Street) „ | 3 35 „ |
| Manchester (London Rd.) „ | 10 55 „ | 6 20 „ | Glasgow (Central)........ „ | 7 50 „ |
| Holyhead (Pier)............arrive | 2 35 a.m. | 10 25 „ | Edinburgh (Princes St.) „ | 7 50 „ |
| {arrive | 5 55 „ | 1 30 a.m. | Chester ........................ „ | 1 54 „ |
| Kingstown (Pier).........{ | | | Bristol (via Birm'gham) „ | 11 37 „ |
| {depart | Thursdays. | Sundays. | Birmingham (New St.) „ | 4 30 „ |
| Queenstown ................arrive | 6 5 a.m. | 1 37 a.m. | London (Euston)............ „ | 6 15 „ |
| | 10 55 „ | 6 15 „ | | |

Through Carriages are run between Kingstown Pier and Queenstown in connection with this Service.

**NORTH WESTERN HOTEL, LIVERPOOL.**—This Hotel situated at Lime Street Station, Liverpool, is lighted throughout by Electricity, and contains upwards of 250 Bedrooms, with spacious Coffee Room available for Ladies and Gentlemen, Ladies' Drawing Room, Reading, Writing, Billiard, and Smoking Rooms. The Hotel is especially appointed for the convenience of American Travellers, as it adjoins the most important Railway Station in Liverpool, from which there are Trains to London (Euston) performing the journey in Four hours and Twenty minutes. Forty minutes Hourly Service of Trains to Manchester, and Through Trains to Leeds, York, Hull, Newcastle, the Lakes, Scotland, Chester, the North Wales Coast, Bristol, Birmingham, Stratford-on-Avon, Oxford, Cambridge, and all parts of England.

Euston Station,
September, 1896.

**FRED. HARRISON, General Manager.**

6

The 'American Specials' were 'special' in that they provided a superior service specifically for passengers travelling between Euston and Liverpool in connection with transatlantic liners. They were not 'special' in the sense of being put on at short notice in response to some unexpected demand, and in fact featured prominently both in the columns of the public timetable and in separate announcements therein, as this extract from the 1896 timetable shows.

# Liverpool Lime Street

*Above* An interior view of Lime Street station in 1866 when it was still under construction, although it seems to be already in use, partially at any rate. The engine is 'Old Crewe Goods' 2-4-0 No 24 *Sirocco*, which was built in May 1854 and is in original condition. Beyond it are four-wheeled carriages, some of which are of very early design - the engine appears to be 'coupled' to the one next to it by means of a rope. The ladder in the centre of the picture seems of record length!

*Right* 'Problem' No 234 *Mazeppa* is awaiting departure with a passenger train, possibly bound for Manchester (Exchange), about 1890. The brass rim to the spectacle frame is well polished, as is the chimney cap; the latter is probably galvanised, a process commonly used at this period to resist corrosion, and since paint did not adhere well to the galvanised surface and soon flaked off, it was easier for the sheds to polish them than repaint them. *Mazeppa* was the name of a Cossack hero in poems by Byron and Victor Hugo; it was also the name of Napoleon's horse.

The station in late 1900, looking over the carriage road from a position above the concourse. On the left an express has just arrived, headed by the first of the 'Experiment' class 2-2-2-0 three-cylinder compounds, No 66 *Experiment*; it is in the same platform as *Mazeppa* in the previous picture. The two leading carriages are Great Western, so the train is possibly the 5.20 pm arrival, which conveyed through carriages leaving Plymouth at 8.30 am. In front of the engine are two open carriage trucks, which have no doubt been so positioned for loading or unloading before the train arrived. Above the engine, in the gap between the columns, is a sign 'COCOA ROOM', while in the distance, on the wall at the right-hand end of the roof, is an advertising hoarding 'SWISS SUITS' (which no doubt incensed many a mill-owner arriving in the city from Lancashire and Yorkshire!). On the right empty suburban passenger trains await their next turn of duty. The numerous horse-drawn vehicles are worthy of close scrutiny. The cart on the right, for instance, is double-headed! Pictures in the Liverpool area are rare, and this is almost certainly the finest picture of Lime Street in LNWR days in existence.

Whale 'Precursor' Class 4-4-0 No 469 *Marmion*, which was built at Crewe in July 1907, at Liverpool (Lime Street) probably soon afterwards.

Facilities at Lime Street were restricted by the fact that the approach to the station was in a deep cutting, but space was somehow found for a turntable on the down side between the platform ends and the cutting. Here, in about 1900, Ramsbottom 'Problem' Class 2-2-2 No 230 *Monarch*, as finally rebuilt by F. W. Webb in September 1898, waits before taking up its return working. The driver and an inspector seem to be discussing some feature of the right-hand cylinder.

A view of Olive Mount Cutting, one of the major feats of construction on the Liverpool & Manchester Railway, looking towards Manchester about 1885. The slow lines and the Bootle branch, coming in on the left, have the ballast covering the sleepers, as was normal for most of the 19th century, but the fast lines on the right have the sleepers visible.

'4 ft Shunter' No 3241 at Edge Hill with a party of visiting enthusiasts. The photograph is thought to have been taken about 1920, shortly before the formation of the North West branch of the Stephenson Locomotive Society. The man on the running plate in the bowler hat is W. H. Whitworth, dentist, special constable and photographer of note, who recorded the LNWR locomotive scene comprehensively with his camera over many years.

*Above* This is something of a puzzle picture. 'Dreadnought' Class three-cylinder compound No 507 *Marchioness of Stafford* is in immaculate condition, probably soon after winning a gold medal at the Inventions Exhibition; F. W. Webb is posing by the front bufferbeam; and the shelter for the Royal Train look-out man is fitted on the tender (his job was to watch for signals from the train telling him that he should instruct the driver to stop). Yet the train is quite ordinary. Except for 30 ft 6 in brake vans front and rear, it consists of assorted 32-foot carriages and was probably used on services between Liverpool and Manchester.

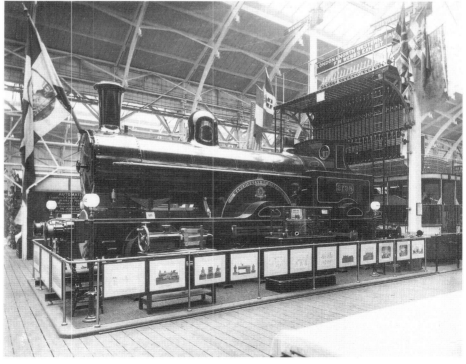

*Right* *Marchioness of Stafford* on display at the Inventions Exhibition in 1885, where it won a gold medal. It is the centrepiece of the LNWR exhibit and carries its Crewe Works motion number, 2798, as was regularly done with LNWR engines displayed at special exhibitions. Beyond it is a signal locking frame beneath the sign 'F. W. Webb's Exhibit'.

*Left* The same train as seen on the previous page on the same occasion, this time at St Helens Junction. Another photograph exists showing the crowd on the far side of the train all looking towards the station out of the picture to the right. Perhaps the Royal Train has just arrived and is to be worked forward by *Marchioness of Stafford*. The humble '17-inch Coal Engine', with its Bickershaw Colliery wagons, appears to have been halted on the bridge so that its crew can observe the proceedings!

*Below left* The first of the '17-inch Coal Engines', No 944, which was built in February 1873, has been specially posed for the official

photographer on a train of locomotive parts. As the location is Earlestown, the locomotives have presumably been built by Vulcan Foundry. The two boilers and tenders are carried on tramcar trolley wagons, but most of the rest of the train consists of small 19th-century wagons with 20-inch or 36-inch sides, many of them being sheeted over. The first wagon is four-plank open No 31527, tare weight 6.0.2. On the left, beyond the engine, is an open wagon loaded with a horse dray. Modellers sometimes wonder how road vehicles were secured on carriage trucks and similar vehicles; in this case the nearest wheel of the wagon is secured by ropes to the wagon buffer.

*Above* At first glance this is another quite unremarkable view of a moving train headed by a '6 ft 6 in Jumbo', but on closer examination it contains much of interest. The train is proceeding along the main line from Manchester to Liverpool and is about to cross over the West Coast Main Line, milepost 16, on the left, being almost on the bridge. In the distance is Parkside No 2 signal box with home signals for Manchester (off), and for Lowton Junction and main line at Golborne Junction. On the front of the engine is the telegraphing number H465; the prefix 'H' was used for trains on the North Wales section in the early 20th century, so as all the carriages are Lancashire & Yorkshire Railway stock the train may well be an excursion from some point on that company's system, such as Bury, Rochdale or Bradford, to Llandudno. If so, the 'Jumbo' has taken over from an LYR engine at Manchester (Victoria), and in view of the load has perhaps been substituted for a larger engine that has failed. It will certainly be banked from Warrington No 1 to Acton Grange.

The most remarkable feature is the stock, which consists of one of the two LYR dining car sets built in 1908-9 for the Liverpool (Exchange)-Hull and Liverpool (Exchange)-York and Newcastle services, but strengthened probably for this working. The first vehicle

is a 56-foot four-compartment Corridor Brake 3rd to D91, of which only six were built for use in these dining car sets. Next come two Corridor 3rds to D90, also built for these sets. The fourth vehicle is something of an oddity, being one of 13 open side-corridor 3rds built at the same time to D97, one of which was also usually to be found in the dining car expresses. They were arranged like any normal side-corridor coach but were open, having no doors leading to the bays of seats, no partitions dividing each bay from the next and no tables in the bays. In later years they were much used in push-and-pull sets, for which they were well suited. In sixth position is a 65 ft 6 in elliptical-roof 12-wheel Kitchen/1st Dining Car, either No 213 or 214, which was normally coupled next to an Open 3rd, so that meals could be served to passengers of that class. In this case the vehicle behind it is not the normal one used for that purpose, which seems to date the picture as during the First World War or later; on the other hand, the low number of the picture in the Locomotive Publishing Company list, 3340, seems to indicate a date well before the war. The remaining coaches are of the same types and variants as those leading. In total the tare weight of this ten-coach train is 278 tons, not bad for an unsuperheated 2-4-0 classified by the LMS as '1P'. No wonder they were nicknamed 'Jumbos'!

# Cheshire and Manchester

*Above* A special train conveying Foden steam wagons for the War Department awaits departure from Sandbach early in the First World War.

*Below* A close-up view of a Foden steam lorry at Sandbach loaded on to a 10-ton wagon that is lettered 'STEAM WAGON TRUCK'. In the wagon diagram book it is described as a 'long deal wagon' of D14. The date is thought to be 1921.

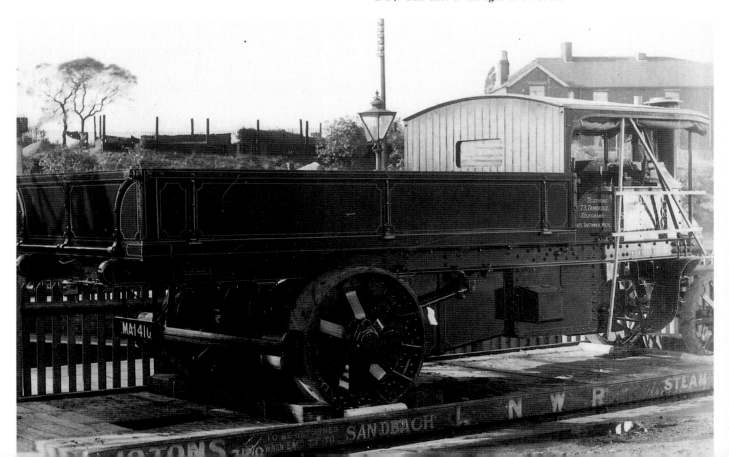

*Above* A very rare view at Cheadle, in the early 1870s. The engine is an 'Old Crewe Goods' 2-4-0, which has been converted to a tank engine and has had its curved nameplate transferred from the driving splasher to the side tank. The first vehicle is a 21-foot Brake Van, the standard type of the 1860s; the others are also vehicles of the mid-1860s, except for the fourth, which is possibly a 27 ft 6 in five-compartment 3rd of 1871-2.

*Below* A horse taxi outside Stockport station around the turn of the century. The inscription on the door seems to read 'Stockport Borough Carriage Company Ltd'.

*Above* A poor picture technically, but a very rare view nevertheless, probably the only one in existence showing a Northern Division Sharp single in service as a tender engine. Originally North Eastern Division No 57, built by Sharp Brothers in 1849, it became 457 when that Division was merged with the Northern Division. The location seems to be Stockport, and the date is between 1863, when the engine was rebuilt and probably received the Ramsbottom safety valves and chimney cap it has in this picture, and 1870, when it was renumbered on the duplicate list.

*Below* Heaton Chapel station, looking towards Manchester (London Road) along the up platform about 1905.

This is a fairly well-known picture, but one that nevertheless is of some interest. It shows Ramsbottom 'DX' No 1080 as originally built in July 1863, with all the early fittings of the day, including Giffard injector and numberplate in the style of a nameplate on the driving splasher. The first carriage is a WCJS 34 feet by 8 feet Lavatory Composite to P19; it has a half 1st compartment with bow end (which is at the other end from that visible). The location is thought to be Manchester (Victoria) before its reconstruction, and the date the late 1860s.

*Above* 'Benbow' Class four-cylinder compound 4-4-0 No 1965 *Charles H. Mason* about 1917. The location has not been positively identified but is believed to be Manchester (Exchange).

*Below* An unidentified 'Jubilee' Class four-cylinder compound 4-4-0 passes Ravensthorpe & Thornhill with an express from Newcastle to Liverpool about 1907. It has come from Leeds via Batley and is about to travel over Lancashire & Yorkshire metals for a short distance through Mirfield before regaining LNWR tracks east of Huddersfield. The 'Jubilees' did good work on this route in the 1900s when displaced from the main line by Whale's 'Precursors' and 'Experiments'.

# North of Preston

The concourse of Fleetwood station, decorated with flowers for some special occasion, about 1905.

Lancaster station: a photograph taken from a down train awaiting departure on 31 July 1924.

*Left* An up express passing Hest Bank double-headed by a 'Jumbo' and a 'Claughton'. The latter is one of the first production batch of nine, as it has the small cut-off of the bufferbeam corner, superheater damper and pyrometer gauge. The date is 1915-17.

*Below left* View of Bolton-le-Sands station, south of Carnforth, in 1900, with both up and down arms on the same slotted signal post.

A general view of Carnforth station about 1910. On the right are the bay platforms and sidings used for parcel traffic and suchlike. To the left of the water column is the main line and beyond that is the Furness Railway side of the station, with platforms for destinations such as Grange and Barrow.

# INDEX